INTRODUCING

Nietzsche

Laurence Gane and Kitty Chan

Edited by Richard Appignanesi

TOTEM BOOKS

First published in the United States in 1998 by Totem Books
Inquiries to PO Box 223, Canal Street Station
New York, NY 10013

Reprinted 1998

Distributed to the trade in the United States
by National Book Network Inc.,
4720 Boston Way, Lanham, Maryland 20706

Originating editor: Richard Appignanesi

ISBN 1 874166 63 3

Library of Congress Catalog Card Number: 97-060793

Printed and bound in Great Britain by
Biddles Ltd., Guildford and King's Lynn

At the front of the intellectual pantheon of the 19th century stand the figures of **Karl Marx** (1818–83), **Sigmund Freud** (1856–1939) and **Friedrich Nietzsche** (1844–1900). Marx's critique of the social-economic system and Freud's analysis of psycho-sexual life have been well assimilated by the late 20th century. The ideas of Nietzsche, however, remain on the horizon of modern consciousness: a disturbing, even frightening, challenge which he knew would not be taken up in his own lifetime. "Imagine a book which speaks of nothing but events which lie outside the possibility of general or even of rare experiences – the first language for a new range of experiences. In this case, **nothing will be heard**!"

Today, more than 100 years later, we are slowly becoming aware of the profound changes in our relationship to truth, science and morality which Nietzsche foretold.

Early Years

On 15 October 1844 in Röcken, Saxony, the Lutheran pastor was blessed with the birth of his first child, Friedrich Wilhelm Nietzsche. The family claimed Polish aristocratic descent, and had produced many generations of clergymen.

Nietzsche's father died of a brain injury following a fall when the boy was only five years old. The next year the family moved to Naumberg. The little boy was introspective and loved poetry and music. At school they called him "the little pastor", and at home he dwelt with his mother, his sister, a grandmother and two aunts. A formative experience, as we shall see!

In 1858, at the age of 14, Nietzsche gained a scholarship to study at the famous Pforta school near Naumberg, a strict Lutheran boarding school of high academic status, where he acquired his love of classical studies. He excelled in Greek and Latin and was devoted to Plato and Aeschylus.

When, in 1864, Nietzsche left Pforta, there was still no hint of the changes to come in his thinking: he thanked his masters and stated his debt of gratitude "to God and the King".

In October 1864, at 20 years of age, Nietzsche entered the University of Bonn to study theology and philology (the literary analysis of classical texts). He soon renounced theology. He explained this in a letter to his younger sister Elizabeth.

IF YOU DESIRE PEACE OF SOUL AND HAPPINESS, THEN BELIEVE; IF YOU WOULD BE A DISCIPLE OF TRUTH, THEN INQUIRE . . .

The next year he moved to Leipzig to follow his favourite professor, Ritschl, who had taken a teaching post at the university.

Schopenhauer: the Denial of Life

At Leipzig, in a second-hand bookshop, Nietzsche discovered *The World as Will and Idea* by the German idealist philosopher **Arthur Schopenhauer** (1788–1860), whose atheism would echo through his own writings.

FROM EVERY LINE
I HEARD THE CRY OF DENOUNCEMENT,
DENIAL AND RESIGNATION; I SAW IN
THE BOOK A MIRROR IN WHICH THE WORLD,
LIFE ITSELF, AND MY OWN SOUL
WERE ALL REFLECTED WITH
HORRIFYING FIDELITY.

For Schopenhauer, like his great predecessor Immanuel Kant, there is a fundamental distinction between the world as it *appears* (**phenomena**) and the world as it truly *is* (**noumena**).

All appearances are mere physical manifestations of an underlying reality, which for Schopenhauer is the WILL.

THUS, BEHIND THE APPEARANCE OF MY BODILY MOVEMENTS LIES THE REALITY OF MY WILL OR DESIRE. THIS WILL DOES NOT EXIST LIKE MY BODY IN TIME AND SPACE — IT IS NOT A PHYSICAL ENTITY AT ALL, BUT UNDERLIES THE WHOLE OF ANIMATE AND INANIMATE NATURE THROUGHOUT THE COSMOS.

This timeless, non-physical cosmic force doesn't lead Schopenhauer to the idea of a God. Instead, Will is seen as the source of all suffering, since willing never brings contentment, but only further desire! (An echo of the teaching of Gautama Buddha.) Thus we are condemned to the endless pursuit of impossible desires: "We blow out a soap-bubble as long and as large as possible, although we well know that it will burst."

This suggests a pessimistic resignation to endure life as best we can. Although Nietzsche later rejected this profound pessimism, Schopenhauer's sombre, atheistic image of a universe moved by blind Will with no ultimate meaning or solace stayed with him.

...THE NEVER-SATISFIED WISHES, THE FRUSTRATED EFFORTS, THE HOPES UNMERCIFULLY CRUSHED BY FATE, THE UNFORTUNATE ERRORS OF THE WHOLE LIFE, WITH INCREASING SUFFERING AND DEATH AT THE END, ARE ALWAYS A TRAGEDY.

SCHOPENHAUER PREACHES ASCETICISM AND THE DENIAL OF LIFE. I SHALL TEACH THE JOYFUL **AFFIRMATION** OF LIFE!

The Scholar as Anti-Scholar

In 1867, Nietzsche was called away from his studies to do military service in the Prussian army. Serving in an artillery regiment, he suffered a bad chest injury while mounting a horse. From childhood, his health had never been good and it was to decline steadily in the future. While convalescing, he began to reflect on the academic way of life and philology in particular. In a letter to his friend Erwin Rhode, 20 November 1867, he writes of ". . . the mole-like activities of the philological brood . . . their indifference to the true and urgent problems of life."

"In the scholar, the instinct of self-defence has decayed; otherwise he would defend himself against books. The scholar is a decadent."

"All writing is useless that does not contain a stimulus to **activity**."

Meanwhile, Nietzsche's early essays on classical Greek culture, published in the *Rheinisches Museum,* brought him to the attention of the authorities at the University of Basel. The following year, 1868, Professor Ritschl received a letter from that university asking if he thought Herr Nietzsche would make a good Professor of Philology.

His teachers at Leipzig decided to award his degree without final examination. Clearly this student was possessed of an unusual intellectual ability.

At Basel, where he taught for the next ten years, Nietzsche became increasingly disillusioned with academic life. This, and his steadily declining health, would lead to his resignation in 1879 at the age of 34. "No entirely radical truth is possible (in academic life)."

The Birth of Tragedy from the Spirit of Music

When his first book *The Birth of Tragedy* appeared in 1872, it served only to distance him from the academic establishment. The only review of it commented: "Anyone who has written a work of this sort is finished as a scholar."

It is easy to see why this book was vilified and dismissed by his colleagues, since it undermines the traditional division between rational-philosophical **discourse** and creative-artistic **expression**, so dear to the Western intellectual tradition. This wonderfully ambitious work seeks to explain . . .

1. The origin of Greek classical tragedy.

2. A fundamental dichotomy in human culture and thought between rational and aesthetic experience.

3. Why the aesthetic form of life is fundamental and the rational is secondary.

4. Why modern culture is sick and how it must be revived.

It achieves its aims using argument, metaphor, anecdote, exhortation, rhetoric and poetic licence, and shows why Nietzsche is the "problem philosopher" for academics: he will not confine his style to orthodox rational expression! Instead, he rattles the iron cage of language, and like the poet Schiller, he believes that "a certain musical disposition of mind comes first, and after that follows the poetical idea."

Apollo and Dionysus

Dionysus, the Greek god of wine, revelry and sensual abandon, represents "primary man". The followers of this cult cast aside language and personal identity to enter an ecstatic dance. Music and intoxication are their means, and "mystical collective ecstasy" is their end.

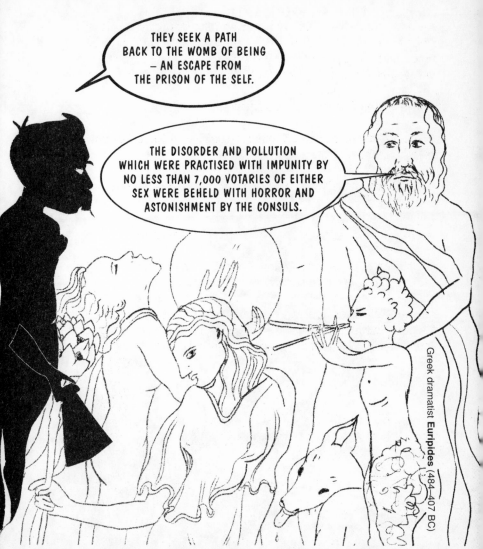

THEY SEEK A PATH BACK TO THE WOMB OF BEING — AN ESCAPE FROM THE PRISON OF THE SELF.

THE DISORDER AND POLLUTION WHICH WERE PRACTISED WITH IMPUNITY BY NO LESS THAN 7,000 VOTARIES OF EITHER SEX WERE BEHELD WITH HORROR AND ASTONISHMENT BY THE CONSULS.

Greek dramatist **Euripides** (484–407 BC)

This trance-like condition briefly protects us from our sense of isolation and the transitory nature of human life, from which our **intuition** won't allow us to escape.

Nietzsche recalls the old legend where King Midas seeks out Silenus, the constant companion of Dionysus, and asks him: "What is man's greatest happiness?" The daemon remains sullen and uncommunicative until finally, forced by the King, he breaks into a shrill laugh.

How did Hellenic culture bear these terrible truths? With the help of another God: **Apollo**.

Apollo, the Sun god of order and reason, embodied in the dream of **illusion**, represents civilized man. The Apolline cult generates optimism. Its insistence on form, visual beauty and rational understanding helps to fortify us against the Dionysian terror and the irrational frenzy it produces. "To be able to live at all, the Greeks had to place before themselves the shining fantasy of the Olympians", with Apollo as their greatest god. Self-control, self-knowledge and moderation: the "middle-path" of the philosopher **Aristotle** (385–322 BC).

Music, the Origin of Myth

Concepts, images and feelings all gain a heightened significance under the influence of music.

DIONYSIAN ART, THEN, AFFECTS THE APOLLONIAN TALENT IN A TWOFOLD MANNER. FIRST, MUSIC INCITES US TO A SYMBOLIC INTUITION OF THE DIONYSIAN SPIRIT, AND SECONDLY, IT GIVES THAT IMAGE A SUPREME SIGNIFICANCE.

Music, then, can give birth to myth, "and above all to the tragic myth which is a parable of Dionysian knowledge".

Music and Tragedy

Nietzsche calls tragedy a "new form of **aesthetic** consciousness" to indicate that the tragic view of life is not just a way of thinking about the world, but first a way of **perceiving** the world, and only **music** can lead us to this perception.

THE DIONYSIAN SPIRIT IN MUSIC MAKES US REALIZE THAT EVERYTHING THAT IS BORN MUST BE PREPARED TO FACE ITS PAINFUL DISSOLUTION. IT FORCES US TO GAZE INTO THE HORROR OF INDIVIDUAL EXISTENCE, YET WITHOUT BEING TURNED TO STONE BY THE VISION.

Only through music can we face the terrible message of Silenus. If classical Greek tragedy has less impact on us today, it is because we experience it only as a stage-play. The music accompanying it has been lost.

The Triumph of Apolline Philosophy

This fundamentally **aesthetic** vision of the primitive world of Dionysus is suppressed by later Hellenic culture which culminates in **Socrates** (469–399 BC).

I DISMISS ALL ART AS SECONDARY IMITATION OF REALITY – A COUNTERFEIT SUBSTITUTE FOR LIFE ITSELF.

THROUGH HIS DISCIPLE **PLATO** (427–347 BC), THE APOLLINE PHILOSOPHY OF OPTIMISM AND BELIEF IN THE POWER OF REASON ALONE WILL HI-JACK THE FUTURE OF WESTERN PHILOSOPHY FOR THE NEXT 2,000 YEARS!

No wonder Nietzsche tells us that modern consciousness is sick: "Art is reduced to **mere amusement**, and governed by empty concepts." The spirit of Dionysus is repressed (Freud will later have something to say about "repression") and we remain cut off from sensual intuition and spiritual truth. The tragic myth has been lost.

The Case of Richard Wagner

Nietzsche found the best contemporary example of the tragic vision in the operas of his friend **Richard Wagner** (1813–83) who, along with the ideas of Schopenhauer, would act as a sounding-board for his own philosophy for years to come. (Finally, he would reject them both.)

In his early years at Basel, Nietzsche became an intimate friend of Wagner and his talented wife Cosima, whom he had first visited at their home in Tribschen in 1869.

Nietzsche at first totally supported Wagner's ideal of a national theatre of the arts at Bayreuth, and devoted much time and energy to the project. His essay *Richard Wagner in Bayreuth* (1870?) heralds Wagner's new Music-Drama synthesis as the rebirth of the golden age of the art of Greece – the saviour of German culture. But, as Nietzsche later realized, he had read into Wagner's work his **own** ideal of art and music.

Wagner considered himself a political and sexual revolutionary, but his socialist optimism could not resist Schopenhauer's profoundly pessimistic philosophy.

When his greatest work *The Ring of the Nibelung* opened at the Bayreuth theatre in August 1876, Nietzsche was dismayed.

I BEGAN BY INTERPRETING WAGNER'S MIND AS THE EXPRESSION OF A DIONYSIAN POWERFULNESS OF SOUL. IN IT I THOUGHT I HEARD THE EARTHQUAKE . . . INDIFFERENT TO THAT WHICH PASSES FOR CULTURE, WHICH WOULD THEREBY BE SHAKEN TO RUINS.

In reality it would be Nietzsche, not Wagner, who would create the major earthquake in the thought of our time.

With the appearance of Wagner's *Parsifal* (1877), Nietzsche's divorce from his former friend was nearly complete, for here Wagner embraces religious symbolism, and the blood of Christ redeems the world!

Nietzsche was beginning to distance himself from Schopenhauer's pessimism. Wagner, on the contrary, "was stuck on the rock of Schopenhauer's philosophy" – his pessimism and resignation – plus a decadent Christianity. This seems undeniable: in a letter to **Franz Liszt** (1811–86), Wagner says . . .

> SCHOPENHAUER . . . APPEARED TO ME IN MY SOLITUDE AS A MESSENGER FROM HEAVEN . . . HIS CENTRAL THOUGHT, THE FINAL NEGATION OF THE WILL TO LIVE, IS OF A TERRIBLE SERIOUSNESS; BUT IT IS **THE ONLY WAY OF SALVATION.**

> WAGNER HAS BECOME PIOUS!

> *LOHENGRIN* CONTAINS A SOLEMN BAN UPON ALL INVESTIGATION AND QUESTIONING. IN THIS WAY, WAGNER STANDS FOR THE CHRISTIAN CONCEPT, "THOU **MUST** AND **SHALL** BELIEVE".

As we shall see, Schopenhauer, Wagner and Christianity will become synonymous for Nietzsche with decadence, weakness, nihilism and the denial of life. The so-called instincts of pity and self-sacrifice become "the great danger of mankind, its most sublime temptation and seduction – seduction to what? To nothingness . . . **the Will turning against life.**"

The break with Wagner was very painful for Nietzsche. "I would not have the days I spent at Tribschen [with him] – those days of confidence, of cheerfulness, of sublime flashes, and of profound moments – blotted from my life at any price."

And yet, finally . . .

I HAD TO SIDE AGAINST ALL THAT WAS MORBID IN MYSELF, INCLUDING WAGNER, INCLUDING SCHOPENHAUER, INCLUDING THE WHOLE OF MODERN HUMANITY.

This increasing sense of isolation, together with a steady decline in his health (constant headaches, failing eyesight) required regular periods of rest and recuperation – cures in spas, journeys to the mountains – while still returning to Basel to teach in term-time.

In 1875 he befriended a young musician, Heinrich Kösehtz – whom he re-named *Peter Gast* (*Gast* in German means visitor, company) – who took dictation of his work and helped to copy his manuscripts.

What is History?

Nietzsche's early work has so far been characterized by a rejection of the rational, scholastic approach of post-Socratic philosophy in favour of the intuitive, libidinal passion of Dionysian art – an aesthetic and life-affirming view of the human condition. However, with the publication of *Human, All Too Human* (1878) we see a more detached and critical side emerging in Nietzsche's thought.

SOCRATIC REASON IS NOW EMPLOYED IN AN INQUIRY WHICH HAS ITS BEGINNINGS IN AN ESSAY . . .

THE USE AND ABUSE OF HISTORY, UNDER THE COLLECTIVE TITLE *THOUGHTS OUT OF SEASON* (1873–76).

Here, the question "What is history?" is given a timely analysis, reflecting on the Prussian military success in Europe in the 1870s.

In 1870, Nietzsche had served briefly in the Franco-Prussian war as a volunteer medical orderly, but he contracted dysentery and diphtheria, requiring long convalescence. He totally rejected the patriotic fervour of the Prussian "Second Reich", seen as a triumph of German cultural ideals in this war.

MODERN PRUSSIA IS A POWER THAT IS ITSELF A DANGER TO CULTURE, JUST AS HISTORY ITSELF CAN THREATEN THE PRESENT BY IDEALIZING GREAT NATIONS OF THE PAST AND EXHORTING US MERELY TO EMULATE THESE DEAD CULTURES.

"We moderns have no culture to call our own. We fill ourselves with foreign customs, arts, philosophies, religions and sciences: we are wandering encyclopaedias." (*Use and Abuse of History*) The point is to **assimilate** the past, to use it in the making of our own life and culture. History is a dead weight on the present.

What is Education?

Education gives us a lot of information **about** culture; its product is the so-called learned person who possesses an excess of history and cannot live an authentic life of his or her own. Education insists on **accurate detail** and **detached "objectivity"** which serve only to paralyze the individual's project of self-realization and action in the world.

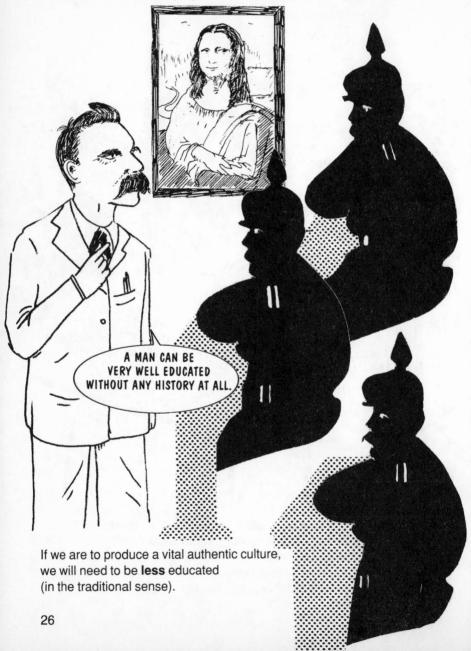

If we are to produce a vital authentic culture, we will need to be **less** educated (in the traditional sense).

What is Culture?

Culture, and the beliefs and values which characterize any group or class, can never be produced by education alone. The greatest peoples sometimes produce **genius**, but this rare event occurs more often in cultures where the State is less involved in the education of its subjects.

Indeed, "All great periods of culture have been periods of political decline." The energy required for politics on a large scale, or in economy, or in universal commerce, or in parliamentarism, or in military interest, usually **reduces** the level of culture of a people.

And how might the dire condition of German culture be improved? Ironically, by those with a healthy disrespect for the status quo, i.e. the youth of the nation. "At first they will be more ignorant than the educated men of the present, for they will have **unlearnt** much and will have lost any desire even to discuss what those educated men especially wish to know: in fact, their hallmark from the educated point of view will be just their lack of science [knowledge], their indifference and inaccessibility to all the good and famous things."

This indifference to history and education will finally produce a genuinely vital culture: a freedom of spirit. "At the end of the cure they are men again and have ceased to be mere shadows of humanities."

Nietzsche, of course, was undergoing this "cure" himself, for only thus could he hope to achieve the radical critique of those "good and famous things" which would revolutionize our modern view of knowledge, morality and human psychology. This questioning of culture will lead to his only teleological* message for us.

So, in the time capsule, we place the greatest treasures of our art and knowledge with our message to the future: if there is value in the life of humans, it lies here in the greatest of cultural works – the rare products of genius.

*Teleology: the theory that processes and events are related to ultimate goals or ends.

A Critique of Metaphysics

If culture is our highest goal, we might ask what becomes of metaphysical theories which speculate on the fundamental nature of reality using reason alone? "It is true, there **could** be a metaphysical world; the absolute possibility of it is hardly to be disputed. We behold all things through the human head and cannot cut off this head; while the question nonetheless remains what of the world would still be there if one **had** cut it off." *Human, All Too Human*

Theories which try to answer this question are simply outside the scope of human investigation. Historically, this question has always had a fascination for philosophers, but what do we gain if we accept the existence of a metaphysical dimension?

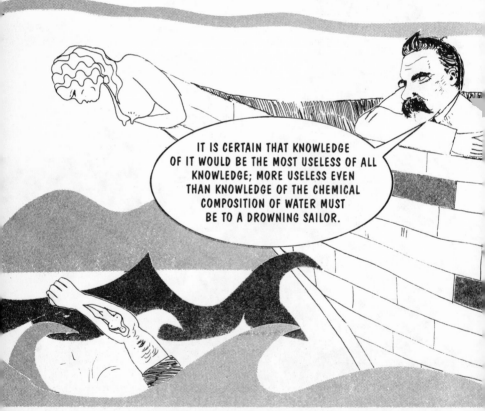

IT IS CERTAIN THAT KNOWLEDGE OF IT WOULD BE THE MOST USELESS OF ALL KNOWLEDGE; MORE USELESS EVEN THAN KNOWLEDGE OF THE CHEMICAL COMPOSITION OF WATER MUST BE TO A DROWNING SAILOR.

And why? Because we are the inhabitants of a physical world; only there do our thoughts and desires have any application. It is in this world of human action that Nietzsche's critical insights will have the greatest impact on the thought of our time.

Kant's Idealism

Here, Nietzsche is taking issue with **Immanuel Kant** (1724–1804), probably the greatest of the German idealist philosophers. Kant epitomizes the tradition of thought going back to Plato which seeks knowledge of final truths beyond the confines of our daily experience: an underlying, timeless reality (like Schopenhauer's idea of Will). This conception of truth wants to transcend the particular facts of any culture or individual, and indeed history itself. Kant describes this domain of timeless truth as **noumena** or "things-in-themselves", opposing it to **phenomena** or "things-as-they-appear" to us through our senses.

Kant's Spectacles

Because we are confined to the use of reason and sensory perception, we can never know the noumenal world. Yet, Kant still insists that such a world exists. He thinks we are excluded from it by our senses, which, like rose-tinted spectacles, present everything to us under various fixed "categories" – time, space, causality – from which we cannot escape.

"Lack of historical sense is the hereditary defect of all philosophers . . . Everything has **become** [what it is]. There are neither eternal facts nor even eternal truths. Therefore what is needed from now on is a **historical** philosophizing, and with it the virtue of modesty." *Human, All Too Human*

Kantian Morality: You Know it Makes Sense

What separates Nietzsche from Kant is the belief in **Becoming**. A need for a fixed and timeless universe makes no sense at all; it is simply "the resentment of the metaphysicians against the real". (This idea of "Becoming" will later produce Nietzsche's maxim "Become what you are" – the notorious symbol of the "Superman".)

Kant offers further offence in his moral philosophy, which formulates the famous **Categorical Imperative**.

> ACT AS IF THE PRINCIPLE OF YOUR ACTION WERE TO BECOME A GENERAL LAW.

> HE BELIEVES HIS MORAL IMPERATIVE IS GUARANTEED BY THE LIGHT OF REASON ALONE – "DO UNTO OTHERS ONLY AS YOU WOULD HAVE THEM DO UNTO YOU." YOU **KNOW** IT MAKES SENSE!

Nietzsche calls this moral fanaticism. It shows Kant's "theologian's instinct". "What destroys [a person] more quickly than to think, to feel without inner necessity, without a deep personal choice, without **joy** – as an automaton of 'duty'?" . . . "A virtue has to be **our** invention, **our** most personal defence and necessity."

This leads Nietzsche to the fundamental point. Morality cannot be based upon reason alone, or if it is, then my reason may not be the same as yours . . .

EACH ONE OF US SHOULD DEVISE **HIS OWN** VIRTUE, **HIS OWN** CATEGORICAL IMPERATIVE. A PEOPLE PERISHES IF IT MISTAKES **ITS OWN** DUTY FOR THE CONCEPT OF GENERAL DUTY . . . KANT'S CATEGORICAL IMPERATIVE SHOULD HAVE BEEN FELT AS MORTALLY DANGEROUS!

Finally, Nietzsche will combine the question of knowledge with the problem of morality – we must not separate them. So we ask not "What can we *know*?", but rather "What is it *good* for us to know?"

Nietzsche's Style

Education, history, culture, metaphysics are just a few of the topics embraced in *Human, All Too Human*. Nietzsche here is developing his characteristically wide-ranging but compressed aphoristic* style: from science and religion to music in a single paragraph! (***Aphorism**: a short, well-expressed, general truth.) Sometimes he is **paradoxical**.

"He who considers more deeply knows that, whatever his acts and judgements may be, he is always wrong."

Sometimes **provocative**.

"There is no pre-established harmony between the furtherance of truth and the well-being of mankind."

Often **polemical**.

"That which we now call the world is the result of a host of errors and fantasies which have gradually arisen in the course of the total evolution of organic nature, have become entwined with one another and are now inherited by us as the accumulated treasure of the entire past."

Even **nihilistic**.

"The irrationality of a thing is no argument against its existence, rather **a condition of it**."

Here, too, he begins to reflect on those topics which will be later developed in *Beyond Good and Evil* (1886), *The Genealogy of Morals* (1887) and *Thus Spake Zarathustra* (1883–5), namely:

1. The Origins of Morality and Religion
2. The Limits of Science
3. The Will to Power
4. The Nature of Truth

Lightness of Touch

Nietzsche's diversity of thought produced a rich, compressed literary style, often using metaphor, simile and parable. He consciously avoided "in-depth" discussion which he considered the trademark of a pedantic academic mind, labouring slowly along a narrow path, in search of absolute truths and a total system of ideas.

I MISTRUST ALL SYSTEMIZERS AND AVOID THEM; THE WILL TO A SYSTEM IS A LACK OF INTEGRITY.

"For I regard profound problems as I do a cold bath – quick in, quick out. That one thereby fails to get down deep enough, fails to reach the depths, is the superstition of hydrophobias . . . Does a thing really remain unintelligible and unrecognized if it is touched, viewed, illumined simply in passing? Does one absolutely have to sit down on it first, to have brooded on it like an egg?" *The Gay Science* (1887)

No; a great thinker possesses a lightness of touch, a freedom of spirit. "Just as the clouds tell us the direction of the wind high above our heads, so the lightest and freest spirits are in their tendencies foretellers of the weather that is coming . . ."

The Aphorism

The scholar's "ant-like industry" produces many a large volume for the reader, confirming in us the assumption that if something is profound it must also be of great length. Nietzsche disagrees: "Something said briefly can be the fruit of much long thought; but the reader who is a novice in this field . . . sees in everything said briefly something embryonic, not without censuring the author for having served him up such immature and unripened fare."

So use words with care and passion – write with blood! Only the most acute reader will grasp the meaning.

"The aphorism, the apophthegm, are forms of eternity; my ambition is to say in ten sentences what everyone else says in a book – what everyone else does **not** say in a book."

Let's examine some aphorisms in action. The subject is "Authors and Readers".

On Authors

"I will never again read an author of whom I suspect that he **wanted** to make a book, but only those whose thoughts unexpectedly **became** a book."

"Real thoughts of real poets always go about with a veil on, like Egyptian women."

"**Q.** Why do you write? **A.** I have found no other way of getting rid of my thoughts."

"Of what account is a book that never carries us away beyond all books?"

"When his book opens its mouth, the author must shut his."

"Paradoxes are only assertions that carry no conviction. The author has made them wishing to appear brilliant, or to mislead, or above all to pose."

On Readers

"A book is made better by good readers and clearer by good opponents."

"Nowadays the text often disappears under the [reader's] interpretation."

"The weakness of modern personality comes out in the measureless overflow of criticism."

"Ultimately, no-one can extract from things, books included, more than he already knows. What one has no access to through experience one has no ear for."

"Somebody remarked: 'I can tell by my own reaction to it that this book is harmful.' But let him only wait and perhaps one day he will admit to himself that this same book has done him a great service by bringing out the hidden sickness of his heart and making it visible."

The Price of Knowledge

With the publication of *Human, All Too Human* Nietzsche's health was shattered. He lost many friends, and a copy of the book which he sent to Wagner received no acknowledgement.

As the future would show, Nietzsche paid the highest price for the "passions of the mind". "If it is your destiny to think, give to it divine honours, and sacrifice to it the best you have and what you love the most." In the next ten years, until the onset of complete mental breakdown in 1889, he would lose many close friends, make enemies and suffer increasing loneliness – all this in addition to almost daily ill health.

EVERY VICTORY ON THE PART OF KNOWLEDGE IS THE RESULT OF HARDNESS TOWARDS ONESELF.

With the house at Basel now closed, Nietzsche will spend the future journeying through France, Italy and Switzerland. 1880 sees him visiting Marienbad, Heidelberg, Frankfurt, Venice, Bolzano, Stresa and Genoa, where he stays the winter. The second part of *Human, All Too Human* is published as *The Wanderer and his Shadow* – an appropriate title for his remaining years . . .

The Eternal Return

In August of 1881, Nietzsche was in Sils Maria, Switzerland.

> I WAS THAT DAY WALKING THROUGH THE WOODS BESIDE THE LAKE OF SILVAPLANA; I STOPPED BESIDE A MIGHTY PYRAMIDAL BLOCK OF STONE WHICH REARED ITSELF UP NOT FAR FROM SURLEI. THEN THIS IDEA CAME TO ME . . .

It was the idea of **Eternal Recurrence**. He was so struck by its power and simplicity that it recurs (!) several times in his future writings. It is very close to the doctrine of the Greek Stoic philosophers, and also echoes the Buddhist idea of Karmic repetition. What is Eternal Recurrence?

We may indeed find such a thought depressing, yet it clearly has a metaphysical comfort too: death is not the end. Although the Christian idea of heaven is clearly more seductive to the seeker after eternal *life*.

Nietzsche and Women

Much has been written about Nietzsche's sexuality: was he homosexual, bisexual, celibate, a woman-hater? The household of his childhood consisted of his mother, grandmother, two aunts and not least, his sister Elizabeth, two years younger than he. His father's death when Nietzsche was only five years old left him subject entirely to women who were devoted to his upbringing and strict training in the Christian values of self-control, meekness, altruism, etc. For a child of Nietzsche's character this must have been hard to bear!

WHEREVER I FOUND THE LIVING, THERE I HEARD ALSO THE SPEECH ON **OBEDIENCE**. WHATEVER LIVES, OBEYS.

As a student he visited a brothel at least once, where he probably contracted syphilis. He never married and had only one love affair that we know of.

In some writings he praises women highly.

"Women have intelligence;
men have character and passion."

"Stupidity in a
woman is unfeminine."

"Is there a more sacred
state than that of pregnancy?"

"The surest remedy
for the male disease of
self-contempt is the
love of a sensible woman."

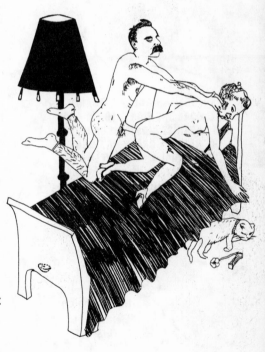

But his critical views
of women predominate.

"Woman is
essentially unpeaceful."

"In revenge and in love,
woman is more barbarous
than man." (Or is this
a compliment?)

"The true man wants two things:
danger and diversion.
Therefore he wants woman,
the most dangerous plaything."

"The perfect woman
tears you to pieces
when she loves you."
(Another compliment?)

"Woman understands children better than man, but man is more childish than woman."

But whatever the differences . . .

So let us say that Nietzsche was:

1. Heterosexual.
2. Probably celibate. (Wagner had written to Nietzsche's doctor suggesting that he engaged in excessive masturbation!)
3. A great admirer of certain women whom he always found problematic: "Man is for woman a means; the purpose is always a child. But what is woman for man?" (Even Freud had difficulty with this question!)

Although Nietzsche had unsuccessfully proposed marriage to a young Dutch woman, Mathilde Trampedach, in 1876, it seems that his only serious love occurred in 1882, for a young Russian girl, Lou Andreas-Salomé (later an intimate of Freud). Nietzsche's friend, the Jewish psychologist Paul Rée, introduced them in Rome, and two days later he proposed to her – again without success! Rée was also in love with Lou, and for a while a *ménage-à-trois* was possible, but soon afterwards Nietzsche lost both his friend and his love.

I SHOULD LIKE YOU BOTH TO PONDER THAT I AM A HEADACHE-PLAGUED HALF-LUNATIC, CRAZED BY TOO MUCH SOLITUDE.

In this state of abandonment, he began his best-known work, *Thus Spake Zarathustra*, in 1883. The figure of Zarathustra, a lonely wanderer in foreign lands, is clearly an image of Nietzsche himself.

50

Lou was clearly a remarkable woman. A photo shows her driving a cart, with Nietzsche and Rée as the horses, whilst she brandishes a whip! Nietzsche's suggestion of a trial marriage ("leasehold") did not in the least scandalize her. She later recalled her first impression of Nietzsche.

The Gay (or Joyous) *Science* (1887) continues Nietzsche's thinking on the critical analysis of culture, begun in *Human, All Too Human*. Here his ideas on science, religion and morality demand nothing less than a new orientation of the modern consciousness.

The Micro-histories of Daily Life

Nietzsche begins with a plea for the study of hitherto "trivial" phenomena. He asks that we turn from the great histories of thought to those events which have an impact on our *daily existence,* and which help to mould it into a particular cultural form. "All that which has given colour to existence has had no history hitherto. Where is there a history of love, avarice, envy, conscience, piety, cruelty? Even a comparative history of justice, or even only punishment, is completely lacking."

THESE HISTORIES, ONCE WRITTEN, WILL SHOW THE GREAT VARIETY OF MORAL CLIMATES PRODUCED BY DIFFERENT FORMS OF LIFE.

THE MORALS OF SCHOLARS, MERCHANTS, ARTISTS, CRAFTSMEN — HAVE THEY YET FOUND THEIR THINKER?

Research will show us that there are **moralities** but not "morality" – no timeless realm where the "goodness" and "truth" of a Plato or a Christ can reign happily forever. This will lead us finally to the hardest of truths concerning morality in *Beyond Good and Evil* (1886), "There are no moral phenomena at all, only a moral interpretation of phenomena . . ."

Is Virtue a Virtue?

For example, let's consider how we regard a person as being **virtuous**. A virtuous (i.e. good) person is praised by others for the good he does *to them*. The virtues – obedience, chastity, justness, industriousness, etc. – will actually *harm* the person who possesses them! "If you possess a virtue . . . you are its victim!" Thus, we praise virtue in others because *we derive advantages from it.*

INSTEAD OF EXPENDING THEIR STRENGTH AND REASON ON THEIR OWN PRESERVATION, EVOLUTION OR ADVANCEMENT – THEY EXPEND IT ON OURS!

NO WONDER VIRTUE IS SO HIGHLY PRAISED – IN OTHERS!

Yet the power of the concept "virtue" remains unchallenged – rather like the idea of "guilt". "Although the most clear-sighted judges of witches and even the witches themselves were convinced the witches were guilty of witchcraft, no guilt in fact existed. So it is with all guilt."

The Power of the Herd

Moral beliefs, then, are always **group beliefs**, and the group is greater than any dissenting individual. "With morality, the individual can only ascribe value to himself as a function of the herd." The herd will later become a central idea in Nietzsche's thinking about the origins of morality. Moral censure and control can only emerge through social consensus.

MORALITY **IS** THE HERD-INSTINCT IN THE INDIVIDUAL.

It represents the power of those who are individually weak but collectively strong. Their moral laws will (they hope) protect them, as well as justify them and the way they live.

The Death of God

If Nietzsche's ideas on the origins of morality are correct – if moral ideas are the simple result of human self-interest and the evolutionary urge to survive – then what can we say of religion, that ancient source of moral principles and commandments? And what will become of our gods? "The whole of religion may appear to some distant age as an exercise and a prelude." Here we encounter for the first time the idea of **the death of God**.

AN AWFUL YET EXHILARATING THOUGHT! AWFUL BECAUSE WE FEEL ABANDONED BY OUR FORMER PROTECTOR, YET EXHILARATING BECAUSE SUDDENLY OUR WORLD OPENS TO INFINITY. ANYTHING NOW IS IMAGINABLE. . .

The "free spirits" among us will feel joy at this news: "Our heart overflows with gratitude, astonishment, presentiment, expectation – at last the horizon seems to us again free, even if it is not bright, at last our ships can put out again, no matter what the danger; every daring venture of knowledge is again permitted; the sea, *our* sea again is there open before us; perhaps there has never yet been such an 'open sea'."

In *The Joyous Science*, Nietzsche puts the news of God's death into the mouth of a madman. People take no notice of him – yet the image is striking: he carries a lantern in the morning, searching everywhere for God who cannot be found.

> WE HAVE KILLED HIM, YOU AND I. WE ARE ALL HIS MURDERERS. BUT HOW HAVE WE DONE THIS? HOW WERE WE ABLE TO DRINK UP THE SEA? WHO GAVE US THE SPONGE TO WIPE AWAY THE ENTIRE HORIZON?

Realizing that no one believes him, the madman considers the bystanders: "I come too early. My time has not yet come. This great event is still on its way, still travelling; it has not yet reached the ears of men . . . This deed is still more distant from them than the most distant stars – **and yet they have done it themselves**." Later that day, he visits the churches in the town and sings a *requiem aeternam deo*. "What are these churches now, if not the tombs and sepulchres of God?"

Life Without God?

Today, over 100 years later, we are still grappling with the consequences of that madman's message. .

A Critique of Science

Nietzsche's thoughts on scientific inquiry are every bit as challenging as his views on morality and religion. Science as an "absolute value" – as a "new religion" for our Godless age – is heavily criticized. The pursuit of knowledge *for its own sake* makes as little sense as the pursuit of goodness *for its own sake*, and can be just as harmful.

If we ask "goodness for what purpose?", so we must also insist on *knowledge for what purpose?* The scientist too often behaves as the *servant* of knowledge; instead, let knowledge be the servant of *man*.

THERE ARE MANY THINGS I DO NOT WISH TO KNOW. WISDOM SETS A LIMIT TO KNOWLEDGE TOO.

If we ignore this warning we will become knowledge-addicts, with dire consequences. "The fact that science as we practise it today is possible, proves that the elementary instincts which protect life have ceased to function." Any truth which threatens life is no truth at all. **It is an error**.

The Methods of Science

Nietzsche sets a further, more radical, criticism against the claim of science to **explain** the world.

> WE CALL IT "EXPLANATION", BUT IT IS "DESCRIPTION" WHICH DISTINGUISHES US FROM EARLIER STAGES OF KNOWLEDGE AND SCIENCE. WE **DESCRIBE** BETTER – WE **EXPLAIN** JUST AS LITTLE AS ANY WHO CAME BEFORE US.

How could we hope to *explain* fire (a change in molecular structure?)

Music (a vibration within a gaseous medium?)

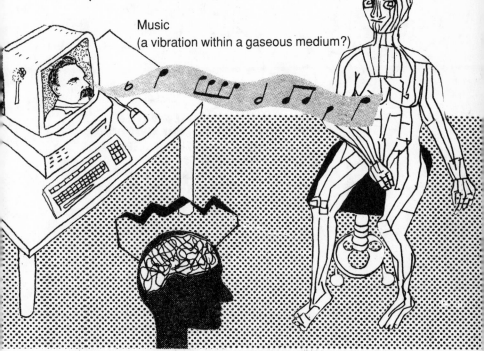

Thought (a change in electrical potential of a biological system?)

What we have achieved are descriptions of greater and greater complexity and sophistication. **But we have explained nothing.** Such phenomena remain as magical to us today as they did to the most primitive human beings.

From Description to Image

We have perfected **images** of how things become what they are – sperm, egg, embryo, etc. – "but we have not got past an image, or behind it".

For example, we describe a **cause** as producing an **effect**, but this is a crude duality, as the Scottish philosopher **David Hume** (1711–76) had pointed out.

So, if we chop up the endless continuum of the world into manageable pieces for our digestion, let us not imagine that the menu we prepare for ourselves is the only, or even the tastiest, one. Yet the hubris of science insists that it is!

"We have arranged for ourselves a world in which we are able to live – with the postulation of bodies, lines, surfaces, causes and effects, motion and rest, form and content: without these articles of faith, nobody could now manage to live!"

60

The Psychoanalysis of Knowledge

Religion, morality, science: their history is "all too human". Their claims to truth fall short of their ambitions. Behind these individual critiques, we can begin to sense a general mistrust of human thought which tends to lack awareness of its deeper motivation and needs. Prefiguring Freud, Nietzsche is beginning to develop a psychological meta-critique of knowledge.

THOUGHTS ARE THE SHADOWS OF OUR SENSATIONS — ALWAYS DARKER, EMPTIER, SIMPLER THAN THESE.

It is ironic that we should take the greatest pride in the most unreliable of our organs. "Consciousness is the last and latest development of the organic, and consequently also the most unfinished and weakest part of it. From consciousness there proceed countless errors which cause an animal, a man, to perish earlier than necessary."

The interleaving of thought with feeling, instinct, desire, need, will provide endless work for the psychologists and analysts of the 20th century and will slowly undermine the simple rationalist belief in "the facts" which still lingers into our own time.

Anti-Darwinian Evolution

The conclusion of this critical period of thinking leads Nietzsche towards the picture of humanity as something only just emerging from its animal past – and still in some ways inferior to the animals. Cut off from our animal instinctual beginnings, with a dangerously over-developed rational faculty – what will become of *Homo sapiens*? Clearly, we are confronting a question of evolution here, but of what kind?

I AM CERTAINLY NOT FOLLOWING THE DARWINIAN IDEA OF "THE SURVIVAL OF THE FITTEST", FOR THIS KIND OF SURVIVAL IS SIMPLY A STRUGGLE FOR **EXISTENCE** – FOR LIFE RATHER THAN DEATH.

The exceptional life-forms may well be poorly adapted to survive. The history of evolving forms shows that: ". . . happy accidents are eliminated, the more highly evolved types lead nowhere; it is the average and below average types which invariably ascend . . ." This simple biological progression is no progress at all – it leads to the victory of the herd.

The Evolution of Quality

Charles Darwin (1809–82) writes in *The Descent of Man* (1871) that a tribe which consisted of many members . . .

. . . WHO WERE ALWAYS READY TO GIVE AID TO EACH OTHER AND TO SACRIFICE THEMSELVES FOR THE COMMON GOOD, WOULD BE VICTORIOUS OVER MOST OTHER TRIBES; AND THIS WOULD BE NATURAL SELECTION.

I WILL REVERSE THIS SCENARIO. LET THE TRIBE SACRIFICE ITSELF, IF NECESSARY, TO PRESERVE THE EXISTENCE OF **ONE** GREAT INDIVIDUAL. IT IS NOT THE QUANTITY BUT THE **QUALITY** OF HUMANITY THAT WE MUST SEEK TO INCREASE.

"A nation is a detour of nature to arrive at six or seven great men. Yes, and then to get round them!" A struggle, not for existence (Darwin), but rather a struggle for **greatness** – and with that, a struggle for **power**. This highly undemocratic view of humanity as a kind of "raw material" out of which a few great individuals will emerge, leads to the question of Nietzsche's political views, which are far from ordinary . . .

Politics: Morality and the State

If the needs of a community, expressed in its morality, are a threat to individual freedom, then we must approach democratic politics with scepticism, for there is a parallel between morality and the law.

Community = morality political democracy = the State

The laws of the State emerge as the morality of the group, writ large.

AS A POLITICAL SUBJECT, IT IS AN ILLUSION TO ASK MYSELF WHAT I REQUIRE FROM THE STATE. IN REALITY, IT IS A QUESTION OF WHAT THE STATE REQUIRES FROM ME.

"Only those who stand outside the political instincts know what they want from the State." *The Greek State* (1873)

The Paradox of Democracy

If my own will happens to coincide with the will of the group, this is just a happy accident, which raises the so-called **paradox of democracy**. In a democracy, I am committed to two principles: 1. The will of the majority (the State); 2. My own will. Unfortunately, there is no necessary reason why these two principles should ever coincide!

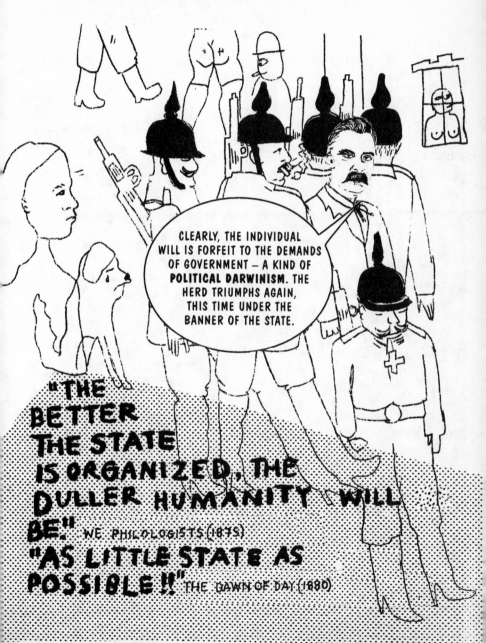

CLEARLY, THE INDIVIDUAL WILL IS FORFEIT TO THE DEMANDS OF GOVERNMENT — A KIND OF **POLITICAL DARWINISM.** THE HERD TRIUMPHS AGAIN, THIS TIME UNDER THE BANNER OF THE STATE.

"THE BETTER THE STATE IS ORGANIZED, THE DULLER HUMANITY WILL BE." WE PHILOLOGISTS (1875)

"AS LITTLE STATE AS POSSIBLE!!" THE DAWN OF DAY (1880)

Invitation to a Political Party . . .

Yet, even today we still preach the doctrine that the State is the most civilized form of society, and our highest duty is to serve it. Nietzsche answers . . .

> WHOEVER THINKS MUCH IS UNSUITABLE AS A PARTY-MAN. HIS THINKING WILL LEAD HIM TOO QUICKLY BEYOND THE PARTY.

With the aid of the aphorism, we can quickly summarize Nietzsche's thinking on the political parties of the day.

Liberalism

"The polite term for mediocre is the word 'liberal'."

"Liberality is often merely a form of timidity in the rich."

Socialism

"There will always be too many people of property [wealth] for socialism to signify anything more than an attack of illness."

"Socialism is the fantastic younger brother of an almost decrepit despotism, which it wants to succeed."

Conservatism

"Conservatives of all times are adventitious liars."

"The doctrine of free will is an invention of the ruling classes."

Politics: the Prostitution of the Intellect

The media representations of our own time – so necessary for political control over entire cultures – were anticipated by Nietzsche. "Is it not necessary for a man who wants to move the multitude to give a stage-representation of himself?" As indeed was the decline in our view of politicians in general. "The robber and the man of power who promises to protect the community from robbers are at bottom beings of the same mould, but the latter attains his ends by different means than the former."

Once again, we are invited to see behind the motives and "ideals" offered by politicians as justification for their political power.

IT IS NOT THE DESIRE FOR POWER THAT I OBJECT TO – THIS IS ENTIRELY NATURAL – BUT THE **MISREPRESENTATION** OF IT THAT IS ENDEMIC TO OUR POLITICAL INSTITUTIONS.

"Politics may one day be found to be so vulgar as to be described, along with all party and daily journalism, under the heading: 'Prostitution of the Intellect'."

Politics: the Death of Truth

Niccolò Machiavelli (1469–1527) had similarly criticized political rulers for their tendency to pass off self-interest as rational, inevitable decision-making. Although his political ideas (he was a staunch republican) are far from Nietzsche's general condemnation of politics, he precedes Nietzsche in his observations on how rulers actually behave, and on their need to act **expediently**. In his *Discourses* (1513–21), Machiavelli wrote this of the Church rulers in Italy.

THE NEARER PEOPLE ARE TO THE CHURCH OF ROME, WHICH IS THE HEAD OF OUR RELIGION, THE LESS RELIGIOUS THEY ARE . . .

Machiavelli's arguments for success in politics lead ultimately to the question of how much power a ruler possesses, and not how much "justice" or "honour" is associated with his cause. The Allied victory in the Second World War shows only that Might prevailed. All sides *always* believe that Right is their ally.

Nietzsche concludes: "The type of perfection in politics is, of course, Machiavellianism." But only if we must have politics at all. "The man with the *furor philosophicus* in him will no longer have time for the *furor politicus,* and will wisely keep from reading the newspapers or serving a party."

Thus Spake Zarathustra

In February 1883, Nietzsche's own *furor philosophicus* reached new heights when, at Rapallo in Italy where he had spent the winter, he wrote the first part of his best-known work, *Thus Spake Zarathustra*, in just ten days.

His intense loneliness, following the Lou Andreas-Salomé affair, is clearly reflected in the character of Zarathustra.

He has a messianic quality, yet rejects those who approach him as disciples. At the end of part four, completed two years later, Zarathustra speaks only to himself.

The title of the book refers to the Sanskrit *Iti vuttakam*, "Thus spake the Holy One". **Zarathustra** or **Zoroaster** (c. 628–551 BC) was a prophet who founded Zendavesta, the religion of Persia before Islam, which survives today in India among the Parsee.

I RECOGNIZE TWO PRINCIPLES – GOOD AND EVIL – PERSONIFIED AS WARRING GODS. GOOD WILL TRIUMPH IN THE END, THE DEAD WILL RESURRECT AND CREATE PARADISE ON EARTH.

IN HIS RELIGION, MORALITY WAS A METAPHYSICAL END IN ITSELF. I CHOSE HIM IN ORDER TO **CORRECT** HIS OWN MISTAKE – AND EXPOSE MORALITY AS A FRAUD!

Zarathustra must now raise his voice not for metaphysics but in the name of the earth, the body, and most of all the Superman.

The Oracle Speaks

The book is a new departure: the anguished outpourings of a being who has arrived at the edge of human affairs. "One must speak with thunder and heavenly fireworks to feeble and dormant senses!" Zarathustra is an extraordinary blend of mystical insight, poetry, yearnings and intuitions.

Truly, a return of the Dionysian spirit! Later, in his autobiography *Ecce Homo* (1888), Nietzsche speaks of his experience of writing *Zarathustra*. "If one had the slightest trace of superstition left in one, it would be hard to deny the idea that one is the incarnation, mouthpiece and medium of almighty powers."

Indeed, it is the work of a poet rather than a philosopher. Although *Zarathustra* is very far from being a philosophical treatise, we can identify three main teachings in it.

It is Zarathustra's task to diagnose present ills and provide direction for a better future.

Although Zarathustra's teachings are the essence of the book, much of the text is devoted to a relentless psychological dissection of modern man, the emptiness of his values and beliefs. This is a picture of a nihilistic, anti-life society which promotes the mediocre and mistrusts originality.

Zarathustra sees around him a general malaise.

Indifference to life (nihilism).

Hypocrisy in morals (and religion).

Fear of the unknown.

On Nihilism

Too much information causes indigestion of the spirit. If we travel far down this road, we shall "choke on our own reason". It is the road to **nihilism**. True knowledge must be **useful** for the projects of human action.

On Virtuous Hypocrisy

The belief of "the virtuous" is a form of hypocrisy. When people say "virtue is necessary", they are really saying "the police is necessary", for what they crave is a quiet, orderly and safe society, where they will be well looked after.

Even worse, they expect a **reward** from their God for being virtuous. Is this a love of virtue?

> BODY AM I ENTIRELY, AND NOTHING MORE; AND SOUL IS ONLY THE NAME OF SOMETHING IN THE BODY!

"The sick and perishing – it was they who despised the body and the earth, and invented the heavenly world and the redeeming blood-drops: but even those sweet sad poisons they borrowed from the body and the earth!" Would the raptures of "heavenly transport" be possible *without a body*?

On Fear

"For today the petty people [the masses] have become lord and master; they preach submission and acquiescence and prudence and diligence and consideration . . ."

Behind this lies a fear of doing, risking and seeking one's own fate. A fear of wanting too much and facing failure.

This modern fear of pain and of suffering shows only that we have not suffered *enough*. All knowledge requires a price.

What is "The Superman"?

Nietzsche's ideas on the evolution of quality prepare the way for the often misunderstood doctrine of the Superman (*Ubermensch* or "over-man"). The term occurs in the work of the Greek satirist **Lucian** (c. 120–180 AD) as *hyperanthropos*, and in part one of *Faust* by **J.W. von Goethe** (1749–1832). It is usually understood in evolutionary terms – an inevitable development towards new life-forms.

BUT THIS IS A DARWINIAN MISUNDERSTANDING OF THE SUPERMAN . . .

Zarathustra sees the Superman as far from inevitable – rather as an extreme challenge to the human spirit. Indeed, the Superman may **never** be realized, but Nietzsche insists that we have an obligation to strive towards such a condition.

Mastery of the Self

Nietzsche sometimes invokes a misleadingly Darwinian image: "What is the ape to man? A laughing-stock or a painful embarrassment. And just so shall man be to the Superman: a laughing-stock or a painful embarrassment."

Yet this "embarrassment" will not be some genetically inferior fossil ancestor. It could instead be the result of change in a single individual's own lifetime.

We can make an ironic comparison with the Christian project of overcoming one's human weaknesses in the quest for salvation of the soul. But in the first pages of the book we are already reminded: "Could it be possible! This old saint in his forest has not yet heard that **God is dead**."

Only the most ambitious project can fill the void left by the death of God – the Superman is the only possible justification left to us.

WHAT IS GREAT IN MAN IS THAT HE IS A **BRIDGE** AND NOT A GOAL; WHAT CAN BE LOVED IN MAN IS THAT HE IS A **GOING-ACROSS** AND A **DOWN-GOING**.

"Down-going" is in German *untergehen*, as in a setting of the sun, a dying, a destroying.

Later, in *The Genealogy of Morals*, Nietzsche will connect the Superman with the "noble" spirit who lives and wills in opposition to the common people who "ask very little of life". Zarathustra has contempt for the ordinary man who "makes everything small. His race is as inexterminable as the flea." Yet to accuse Zarathustra of inhumanity is to miss the point.

A Human or Post-Human Future?

Zarathustra's recurring fear is that the time is not right for his teachings: "The mob could become master, and all time be drowned in shallow waters." The doctrine of the Superman is perhaps as frightening to us today as it was in 1883. If so, then the shopkeepers shall inherit the earth!

> THEY CRUCIFY HIM WHO WRITES NEW VALUES ON NEW LAW-TABLES, THEY SACRIFICE THE FUTURE **TO THEMSELVES** – THEY CRUCIFY THE WHOLE HUMAN FUTURE!

And thus, we the people (you and I?) will hold on to our happiness, our comforts and our gods. A weariness of spirit afflicts us, "a poor ignorant weariness, which no longer wants even to want: that created all gods and afterworlds."

The Will to Power

Clearly, the challenge of the Superman requires an attitude of mind which Nietzsche found lacking in his own culture. Such an attitude requires an extraordinary level of courage. Zarathustra calls this **the Will to Power**. Nietzsche had encountered this idea in Schopenhauer.

THE FUNDAMENTAL DRIVE IN ALL CREATURES IS THE WILL TO LIVE.

YET BEYOND THIS WILL MAY LIE ANOTHER IMPULSE.

Any creature that deliberately risks its life for any reason is denying the "will to live". In such a situation, that creature shows something more

Superficially, the idea of the Will to Power suggests a crude principle – the victory of the strongest. But fundamentally, it is a psychological principle of human behaviour that every being seeks to extend its sphere of action and influence: to consolidate itself.

In the section "Of Self-Overcoming", Zarathustra says: "The will of the weaker persuades it to serve the stronger; its will wants to be master over those weaker still: this delight alone it is unwilling to forgo."

AND AS THE LESSER SURRENDERS TO THE GREATER, THAT IT MAY HAVE DELIGHT AND POWER OVER THE LEAST OF ALL, SO THE GREATEST, TOO, SURRENDERS AND FOR THE SAKE OF POWER STAKES – **LIFE** ITSELF.

The greater the will, the higher the stakes, and even the weakest can "steal by secret paths into the castle and even into the heart of the

Self-Obedience

Strength of will can overcome the greatest power of arms, yet the hardest overcoming will be the **overcoming of itself**: "He who cannot obey himself will be commanded."

. . .COMMANDING IS MORE DIFFICULT THAN OBEYING . . . FOR THE COMMANDER BEARS THE BURDEN OF ALL WHO OBEY, AND THAT BURDEN CAN EASILY CRUSH HIM.

Difficult also because the Will to Power must find within itself its **own** reasons for what it does, not those of another. No wonder Nietzsche calls this philosophy "strenuous" – for together with the total responsibility for every action goes the requirement of creating one's own **value** for that action.

The Free Spirit

Clearly, the higher man or "free spirit" who can totally embody the Will to Power is a being not yet seen, although Nietzsche contends that certain historical individuals do approach that ideal – Julius Caesar, Goethe, Napoleon.

Critics usually see in these doctrines the picture of a selfish, egotistical, unscrupulous and self-serving individual. But Nietzsche will not allow this as counting against his position.

AT THE RISK OF DISPLEASING INNOCENT EARS, I SUBMIT THAT EGOISM BELONGS TO THE ESSENCE OF A NOBLE SOUL . . . AND HAS ITS BASIS IN THE PRIMARY LAW OF THINGS.

Concerning the accusation of "self-serving", he might reply, "Who else should we wish to serve, if not ourselves?" Here, as elsewhere, we see his old opponent Christian ethics (our ethics?) under the microscope.

The Circle of Time

Zarathustra's third doctrine – the eternal recurrence of things – shows a more human (rather than superhuman) side to his character, since it offers a metaphysical solace to our feelings of abandonment at the loss of our gods.

In "Of the Vision and the Riddle", Zarathustra describes two roads.

The portal is inscribed "The Moment". An eternity lies behind him, and an eternity yet again lies before him; an unending chain of events in which he is inextricably involved.

A Pessimistic Consolation

If "eternal recurrence" offers us the promise of an eternity, it is not one with a "happy ending" – for it offers no ending at all. Like the punishment of Sisyphus in the Greek myth, we are condemned to a terrible repetition of events for all eternity. This lack of purpose or ending – a form of meaninglessness which echoes the "endless desiring" in Schopenhauer's philosophy – adds a pessimistic undertone to Zarathustra's otherwise joyful preachings.

Here again we find an emphasis on "the moment" – on our present **action** and **will** – and whatever follows is tied to this for all eternity.

BUT WHERE SCHOPENHAUER PREACHES RESIGNATION, I TEACH DEFIANCE, FOR THE SUPERMAN AND THE WILL TO POWER ARE PRIMARILY **LIFE-AFFIRMING** DOCTRINES.

Wagner's Shadow

Shortly after completing parts one and two of *Thus Spake Zarathustra,* Nietzsche received news of Richard Wagner's death. For the rest of his own life, he would wrestle with Wagner's ghost.

In a letter to Peter Gast, he tells how hard it was to be the enemy of the man he had most revered. Although ultimately insincere in his desire for greatness, Wagner nevertheless embodied virtues of the "higher man". Despite Wagner's anti-Semitism, his Christianity and his infidelities, Nietzsche could never entirely give him up. His death served only to increase Nietzsche's sense of isolation from the world.

The Germans and the Jews

By now, all thoughts of returning to live in Germany were abandoned. The following year, 1884, Nietzsche met his sister in Zürich.

Increasingly, Nietzsche identified every kind of folly with the German character, and frequently defended the Jews against German racism. "The Jews are beyond all doubt the strongest, toughest, and purest race at present living in Europe."

It is folly, he says, to sacrifice the Jews as the scapegoats of all possible public misfortunes. This he calls the "genetic fallacy" – to judge a person on their origins rather than on their actions. He observes that "Every nation, every individual, has unpleasant and even dangerous qualities. It would be cruel to require the Jews to be an exception."

Of Jewish culture, he says: "The Jews, with Heinrich Heine and Offenbach, approached genius in the sphere of art." But Jewish morality, along with Christianity, he criticized severely.

Anti-Germany

The Germans provide ample material for Nietzsche's love of the aphorism.

IN GERMANY, BAD WRITING IS LOOKED ON AS A NATIONAL PRIVILEGE.

A GERMAN IS CAPABLE OF GREAT THINGS, BUT HE IS UNLIKELY TO ACHIEVE THEM, FOR HE OBEYS WHENEVER HE CAN, AS SUITS A NATURALLY LAZY INTELLECT.

GERMAN INTELLECT IS INDIGESTION.

THE FEW INSTANCES OF HIGHER CULTURE I HAVE MET IN GERMANY WERE FRENCH IN ORIGIN.

THE GERMANS HAVE A GREAT KNOWLEDGE OF CULTURE, BUT THEY ARE NOT CULTURED.

WHEREVER GERMANY EXTENDS HER INFLUENCE SHE RUINS CULTURE.

EVERY GREAT CRIME AGAINST CULTURE DURING THE LAST FOUR CENTURIES LIES ON THE CONSCIENCE OF THE GERMANS.

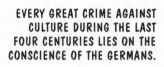

If such remarks had been collected in a single volume, no doubt the Nazis would have burnt it.

95

Beyond Good and Evil (1885–6)

This book summarizes Nietzsche's relentless campaign against the "eternal idols". We should know by now which "idols" he means. In *Twilight of the Idols* (1888), he speaks of "philosophizing with a hammer **as with a tuning fork**" to test the hollowness of these eternal idols.

Although *Beyond Good and Evil* covers the breadth of Nietzsche's interests, we shall use it primarily as an introduction to his later far-reaching analysis of morality, *The Genealogy of Morals* (1887).

The Dishonesty of Philosophy

As soon as the word "truth" is mentioned, philosophers begin to make "a mighty and virtuous noise". This is unsurprising, given the Greek meaning of "philosopher" (*philo* = lover [of] *sophia* = wisdom, truth). Yet this special proprietary relation to truth which philosophers claim is really unjustified.

Philosophers believe that their theories are produced through a dispassionate, objective and rational process – a "cold, pure, divinely unperturbed dialectic" which they like to contrast with the subjective, unreliable efforts of mystics and others.

In reality, however, philosophers' thinking is always preceded by a desire, a prejudice, an inspiration or "desire of the heart" – that is, an irrational need or belief which they proceed to make abstract and defend with reason. Or as the French mathematician and philosopher **Blaise Pascal** (1623–62) nicely put it . . .

Kant, with his "dialectical by-paths", and **Baruch Spinoza** (1632–77) with his geometric methods and formulae, are both at bottom "old moralists and moral-preachers". Nietzsche does not want to imply that philosophy can ever perform more than this limited activity. He simply wants philosophers to recognize the true nature of their "inquiries".

$$E(ax+by = \sum(az, +by).h(x,y)$$

GREATER SELF-KNOWLEDGE WILL NOT LEAD TO MORE VALID THEORIES, BUT IT WILL AT LEAST GIVE US A CLEARER PICTURE OF WHAT WE ACTUALLY DO WHEN WE PHILOSOPHIZE.

Or as the English philosopher **F.H. Bradley** (1846–1924) said: "Metaphysics is the finding of bad reasons for what we believe upon instinct."

99

Here we find Nietzsche's clearest exposition of the religious nature and the purpose of organized religion (Christianity, Buddhism, etc.). For the word "nature", we can substitute "neurosis", for Nietzsche sees nothing natural in religion.

THE RELIGIOUS NATURE FOLLOWS THE PATH OF **SELF-DENIAL**, USING SOLITUDE, FASTING AND SEXUAL ABSTINENCE.

History has seen numerous religious "epidemics" (e.g. the Inquisition, fundamentalism), but the affliction has always existed at some level!

Its greatest phenomenon is **the saint**, whom even the greatest rulers have respected. They rightly see in the saint the force of a most powerful will – so strong that it can bear the greatest self-denial ever seen.

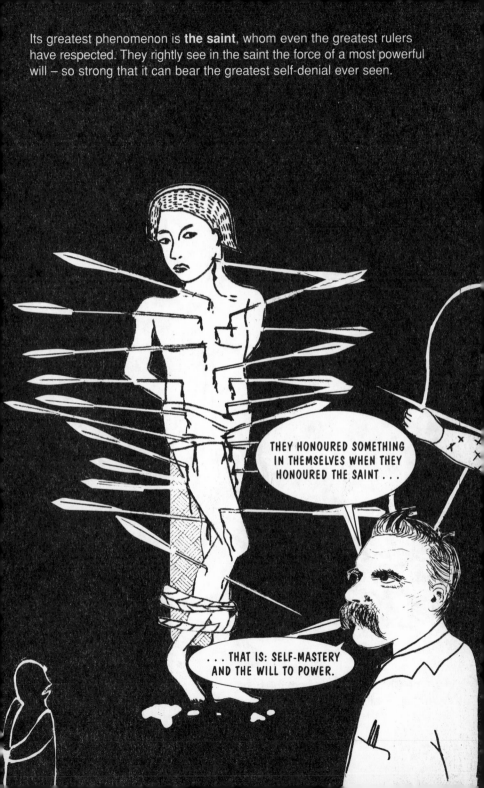

Of Faith

What is the "faith" which religion demands of us? Nietzsche answers this question with the example of Pascal, whose religious belief placed severe restrictions on the scope of his intellectual work.

"The Christian faith is from the beginning sacrifice: sacrifice of all freedom, all pride, all self-confidence of the spirit, and at the same time enslavement and self-mockery, self-mutilation."

The Danish philosopher **Søren Kierkegaard** (1813–55) had called faith a "divine madness", an "absurdity" requiring a "leap" over our faculty of reason. He is another of Nietzsche's targets.

Making the Most of Suffering

Ironically, we find praise for religion when it serves the common man.
The majority of humanity will find great consolation in religious teachings.

On the Natural History of Morals

Nietzsche was preparing the ground for his *Genealogy of Morals* (1887). In a series of acute observations, he catalogued the phenomena which have, over the millennia, given rise to our present conception of morality. He identified a **pre-moral** condition, brought about through the fact of group or social living, which is worth quoting in full.

". . . ever since there have been human beings there have also been human herds (family groups, communities, tribes, nations, states, churches), and always very many who obey compared with the very small number of those who command – considering, that is to say, that hitherto nothing has been practised and cultivated among men better or longer than **obedience**, it is fair to suppose that as a rule a need for it is by now innate as a kind of **formal conscience** which commands: Thou shalt unconditionally do this, unconditionally not do that, in short 'Thou shalt'. This need seeks to be satisfied and to fill out its forms with a content: in doing so it grasps about wildly, according to the degree of its strength, impatience and tension, with little discrimination, as a crude appetite, and accepts whatever any commander – parent, teacher, law, class prejudice, public opinion – shouts in its ears."

The Ruler as Servant

Nietzsche points out that those commanding will usually hold their authority over the group by claiming to represent a *higher* authority still – ancestors, justice, the law or even God. Frequently, a good deal of self-deception or bad faith is involved. Queen Elizabeth II is Britain's "defender of the faith". President Clinton in the USA is "the first servant of the people".

IN REALITY, THE OPPOSITE IS TRUE: THE HERD IS COMMANDED, BUT PREFERS TO THINK OTHERWISE AT THE LEVEL OF CONSCIOUSNESS.

Evil

Nietzsche's final aphorisms are also to be found in *Beyond Good and Evil*. Despite the title, the concept of "evil" is not central to his thought at this time. It is inextricably linked to the Christian morality: an earlier (pre-moral?) age would have no use for the idea.

THAT WHICH AN AGE FEELS TO BE EVIL IS USUALLY AN UNTIMELY AFTER-ECHO OF THAT WHICH WAS FORMERLY FELT TO BE GOOD – THE ATAVISM* OF AN OLDER IDEAL.

NIETZSCHE'S IDEA OF ATAVISM INFLUENCED MY BREAKTHROUGH PAINTING OF 1907, "LES DEMOISELLES D'AVIGNON", WHICH LED TO CUBISM.

Thus magic, godlessness, the worship of false gods (Satanism?), irrational behaviour (schizophrenia?), eroticism – have all been classed as "evil" phenomena from the group viewpoint at one time or another. This is because they elevate the individual above the group, thus threatening the majority. Let that which is a threat be called evil!

*Atavism: reversion to an earlier type.

Some of Nietzsche's most profound psychological aphorisms and maxims in this work are also formulated here. They do not always permit a single interpretation.

On Madness

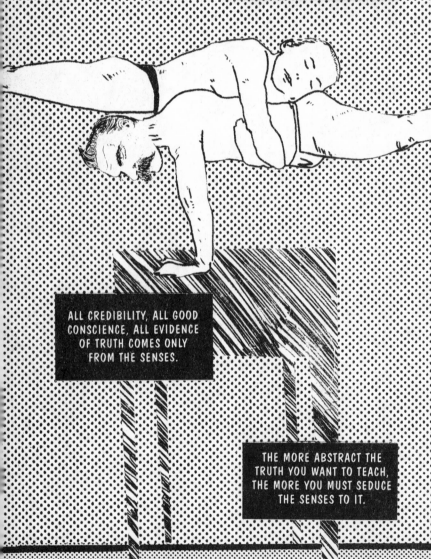

ONE NO LONGER LOVES ONE'S KNOWLEDGE ENOUGH WHEN ONE HAS COMMUNICATED IT.

ALL CREDIBILITY, ALL GOOD CONSCIENCE, ALL EVIDENCE OF TRUTH COMES ONLY FROM THE SENSES.

THE MORE ABSTRACT THE TRUTH YOU WANT TO TEACH, THE MORE YOU MUST SEDUCE THE SENSES TO IT.

We have already seen Nietzsche's most famous aphorism on morality . . .

"There are no moral phenomena at all, only a moral interpretation of phenomena . . ."

The reverberations of this radical proposition still echo today and reappear in several ways. To scientific atheism, it suggests that only the material or physical world can be studied and known.

MORALITY IS NONSENSICAL. OR AS WITTGENSTEIN PUT IT . . .

THERE ARE NO PROPOSITIONS OF ETHICS.

TO RELIGIOUS PEOPLE, IT SUGGESTS THAT NIETZSCHE IS AN AGENT OF THE DEVIL!

To psychoanalysts, following the teaching of **Jacques Lacan** (1901-81), it raises the question of the **desire** of the subject who speaks.

ALL INTERPRETATION REQUIRES A **DESIRE** AT ITS BASE.

If we stay closer to Nietzsche and ask why he wants to deny "moral phenomena" any factual status, we are reminded of his insistence that **any** moral system has a practical aim – to control human behaviour.

ALL MORALITY IS **PARTISAN**. JUST AS ANY LEGAL SYSTEM WILL FAVOUR CERTAIN BEHAVIOUR AGAINST OTHERS.

WHEREAS WE REGARD PHENOMENA AS **INDEPENDENT** OF HUMAN THOUGHT.

Certainly, our thought will attempt to shape the phenomena as they appear (producing a human view of the world), but Nietzsche insists that we do not take this product of our efforts as having any objective status of its own. Hence, "there are no moral phenomena".

The Master and the Slave

Nietzsche has by now identified a central rift in the history of moral feeling, between those who accept and obey a moral code (and welcome it for their own self-protection), and those (rarer individuals) who will accept no authority but their own. These groups have a symbiotic relationship as **master** to **slave**. Nietzsche points out that such a division is never total. Indeed, aspects of both can co-exist unhappily (?) within a single individual. This denies the classical master and slave relation proposed by the philosopher **G.W.F. Hegel** (1770–1831) which sees both terms as mutually exclusive.

I SUGGESTED THAT THE SLAVE GRADUALLY MOVES TOWARDS INDEPENDENCE OF THE MASTER.

NO, THE OPPOSITE IS TRUE!

In Nietzsche's view, the slave mentality deepens and perfects itself over the millennia in an ever more implacable resistance to the master. This resistance will never overcome that "will-to-power" which the truly "free spirit" possesses.

Noble Ethics

The prototype of the "free spirit" in ethics finds its origins in aristocratic cultures such as that of Ancient Greece. Here the idea of "good" is associated with ". . . exalted, proud states of soul which are considered distinguishing and determine the order of rank" (i.e. the social order).

In such cultures, there exists no idea of **good/evil**, but rather **noble/ignoble**. These terms are applied to people, not actions.

But Nietzsche is at pains to point out that simply to be born into the aristocratic class does not guarantee exceptional character! This would be another case of the genetic fallacy (see page 93). This ethic is fundamentally **self-creating**: "The noble type of man regards himself as a determiner of values." We may also call this the ethics of the Master.

Slave Ethics

Slave ethics, which Nietzsche explores more fully in *The Genealogy of Morals*, represents the ideas of "good" and "bad" quite differently.

Ultimately the choice is a simple one. We either make our values for ourselves or we observe (unwillingly) the values of others. Historically, the slave ethic has predominated, but we occasionally find the will to transcend it, and thus to go "beyond good and evil".

The Man Apart

Nietzsche's books went virtually unread in Germany in his lifetime. He could find no publisher for the fourth part of *Zarathustra* ("A Book for All or No One", finished in early 1885), so he paid himself for the printing of 40 copies. Even then, he could find only seven people to whom he could send copies! As late as 1888, he complained to his friend Baron von Seydlitz ...

By then, Nietzsche's writings were beginning to find sympathetic responses in France and Scandinavia, but he felt more friendless than ever. In a letter to his sister Elizabeth, he said: "A profound man needs friends, unless he has a God. I have neither God nor friend."

In another letter of 1888 to his sister, Nietzsche speaks with a lofty and isolated sense of his mission. "You do not even seem to be remotely conscious of the fact that you are the next of kin to a man whose destiny is to decide the fate of millennia – speaking quite literally, I hold the future of mankind in my hand . . ."

An old fellow-student, Erwin Rhode, now a celebrated professor of philology at Leipzig, commented on these last crucial years before Nietzsche's final collapse.

Nietzsche had become addicted to a mysterious Javanese drug (opium?) which he took to relieve his increasing pain and sleeplessness. In this deplorable condition, he wrote his most influential work, *The Genealogy of Morals*, in just fifteen days in the summer of 1887.

The Genealogy of Morals

In the preface to this extraordinary work, we are reminded that of all the knowledge that we seek, the hardest by far to achieve is **self-knowledge**. The axiom, "Each man is farthest from himself" seems forever true, yet Nietzsche's most consistent motivation is always towards the overcoming of this "last frontier" of knowledge.

In this context, *The Genealogy of Morals* represents a major step in our understanding of human psychology, since its avowed aim is nothing less than to expose the creation of value itself.

This is a twofold project.
1. A history and analysis of moral ideas. This in turn is underpinned by:
2. A critique of psychology – *how* could human beings have arrived at these moral principles?

Of this book, Nietzsche later said that it contained ". . . very unpleasant truths, becoming audible as a dull mumbling in the distance." And it is easy to see why later psychologists would follow Nietzsche's principle of suspicion. Never accept human reasoning at face value, for it seeks to mask what it fears to confront: some "very unpleasant truths".

The Ethics of Pity

Nietzsche's suspicion is first turned towards what he calls the "non-egotistical instincts" – compassion, self-denial and self-sacrifice – for in these qualities he senses "stagnation, nostalgic fatigue, and a will that has turned **against** life". (The *ennui* or anti-life feeling expressed in these qualities leads to **nihilism** which he likens to a seriously debilitating disease.)

AMONG THE "NON-EGOTISTICAL" QUALITIES, I SINGLE OUT **PITY** AS THE FUNDAMENTAL "ANTI-LIFE" INSTINCT, FOR IN PITYING ANOTHER WE WEAKEN OURSELVES. NOR DO WE IN ANY WAY BENEFIT THE OBJECT OF OUR PITY.

Pity works against the development of humanity because it attempts to preserve what is ripe for destruction (reflecting perhaps our general fear of death – even the death of the weakest).

Our contemporary moral debates and battles over euthanasia, abortion and medical pathologies of every type all centre around the question of the value of pity.

From the Victorian love of "good works" and Charitable Trusts, to Amnesty International and Band Aid, we see everywhere in Western societies the **ethic of pity** at work.

Of course, Western readers will hardly need to be reminded that pity is also a cornerstone of the Christian religion.

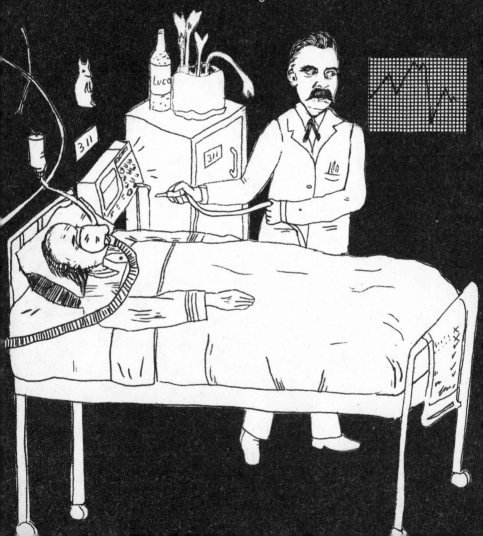

The Slave Revolt in Ethics

Nietzsche's observations on "pity" lead to the inescapable conclusion that this moral value is actually *harmful* to our psychological well-being, yet is central to the moral thought of modern "civilized" societies!

THE HIGH ESTEEM GENERALLY PLACED UPON SUCH AN ANTI-LIFE VALUE REPRESENTS THE TRIUMPH OF **SLAVE ETHICS** — THE MORALITY OF THE WEAKER, OPPRESSED MAJORITIES OF HISTORY.

This revolt reaches back to the origins of Judaeo-Christian thought. Its leaders are the priestly caste, whose achievement consists in the triumph of the human ability to rationalize misfortune and repress instinctual needs. A fundamentally **intellectual** triumph.

The Sins of the Fathers

Nietzsche is tough on the priests, whom he sees as the greatest, but also the most intelligent **haters** in history. As the leaders of a weaker majority, their ability does not lie in strength of arms; instead they must rely on their mental powers.

IT IS THEIR PHYSICAL IMPOTENCE WHICH MAKES THEIR HATE SO VIOLENT AND SINISTER, SO CEREBRAL AND POISONOUS.

The vengeance of such a caste will be the most brilliant vengeance of all! Yet the paradox here is that only through the priestly caste has human intelligence, subtlety and profundity been able to develop. It is on the soil of priestly existence that some of the finest creations of the human intellect have blossomed!

Slave Ethics: the Inversion of Values

Perhaps the most original act of the priestly caste was the creation of a new system of values. By a process of inversion, they took the noble values of their rulers (the strong and powerful) and turned them into their opposite – the great vices or "sins".

The Idea of Evil

Once this priestly **transvaluation** is accomplished, it is a short step to the complete rejection of noble ethics.

In this rejection of the values of noble ethics the priestly caste develop a further brilliant device – the idea of **evil**.

BOLDNESS IS REALLY ARROGANCE . . .

PRIDE IS REALLY SELF-LOVE, ETC., ETC.

PSYCHOLOGICALLY, WE FIND HERE THE IDEA OF REPRESSION: THE REFUSAL TO ADMIT TO DESIRING WHAT ONE CANNOT OBTAIN. BETTER TO REJECT IT AS WORTHLESS!

The lines of opposition between noble and slave ethics now clearly emerge.

... ONLY THE POOR, THE POWERLESS, ARE GOOD; ONLY THE SUFFERING, SICK, AND UGLY, TRULY BLESSED. BUT YOU NOBLE AND MIGHTY ONES OF THE EARTH WILL BE, TO ALL ETERNITY, THE EVIL, THE CRUEL, THE AVARICIOUS, THE GODLESS, AND THUS THE CURSED AND DAMNED!

THE SIMPLE VALUES OF THE NOBLE SPIRIT CONTAIN THE IDEA OF BAD ALMOST AS AN AFTER-THOUGHT. NOBLE MORALITY DEVELOPS PURELY FROM SELF-AFFIRMATION – SAYING "YES" TO LIFE.

Noble ethics grows spontaneously from the fulfilment of its will and action in the world. Its central concept is "Good". The ancient Athenian rulers often described themselves as "we noble, good, beautiful, happy ones". In such a context, "Bad" means simply the lack of life-affirming qualities.

The Rancour of the Weak

Thus in the noble ethic, "Bad" is simply a lack, appended to the central idea of "Good". In slave ethics, the ruling concept is "Bad", which it re-names evil. Slave ethics begins by saying no to an "outside", an "other", a non-self, and that **no** is its creative act.

Nietzsche finds the origins of the slave ethic in the **rancour** of the weak who, unable to carry out their will and thus deprived of an outlet for action, indulge in an imaginary vengeance and denigrate what they cannot emulate.

Two Views of the Enemy

These two moralities perceive their enemies quite differently.

The noble person **respects** his enemy, whom he needs as a foil for his own willing and action, and "respect is already a bridge to love".

The enemy conceived by the slave ethic – the rancorous spirit – is a being quite unlike himself.

In this slave ethic we see a profound self-deception: "The rancorous person is neither truthful nor ingenuous nor honest and forthright with himself. His soul squints, his mind loves secret paths and back doors . . ." Yet such a person will be cleverer than the noble or aristocratic person – more scheming – living "by his wits". But finally, he represents "the smell of failure, of a soul that has gone stale" – a high price to pay for reason and the repression of emotion.

The Origins of Conscience

Nietzsche deplores the fact of human conscience, and along with it, the phenomenon of **guilt** or bad conscience. (**Conscience**: inmost thought, particularly concerning the sense of right and wrong. Q.E.D.)

We may regard conscience as a peculiarly human characteristic, but *The Genealogy of Morals* suggests that it is a comparatively recent development in the history of human psychology. It coincides with the beginnings of social structure and law-making, which in turn depend on the repression of **instinct** and the development of **rationality**.
This jump in evolution, a movement away from our animal nature towards *Homo sapiens* (from the Latin, "wise man") has been the cause of our greatest unhappiness.

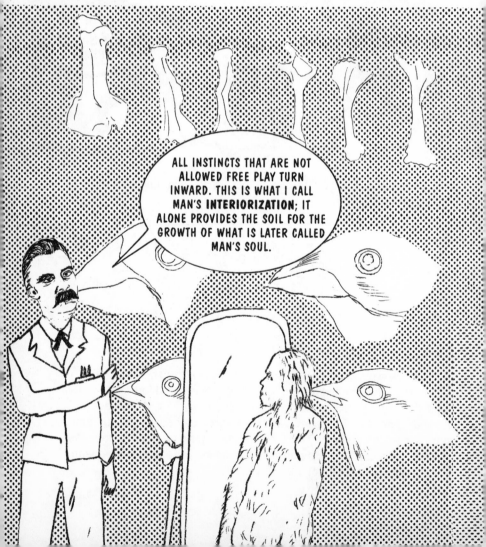

Just as the free-swimming sea-creature forced to leave its natural habitat and adapt to land, finds its new condition awkward and clumsy, so do we find our newly acquired "moral sense" a burden which impedes our former freedom of action. This "declaration of war" against our old instincts is unhealthy.

A daily war of attrition between instinct and morality – the "gnawing of conscience" – becomes the state of normality.

The Disease of Consciousness

Nietzsche deeply admired the Russian novelist **Fyodor Dostoyevsky** (1821–81). "Here you have a psychologist with whom I am in agreement", he wrote to Peter Gast in 1880. He refers in another letter (7 March 1887) to Dostoyevsky's novella, *Notes from the Underground* (1864), a confession of astounding and frightful insights. The unnamed anti-hero of this story plumbs the depths of misery and paralysis which comes from the illness of self-consciousness: "I am a sick man. I am a spiteful man. I am an unattractive man. I believe my liver is diseased . . ."

I WANT NOW TO TELL YOU, GENTLEMEN . . . WHY I COULD NOT EVEN BECOME AN INSECT! . . . TO BE CONSCIOUS IS AN ILLNESS . . . FOR MAN'S EVERYDAY NEEDS, IT WOULD HAVE BEEN QUITE ENOUGH TO HAVE . . . HALF OR A QUARTER OF THE AMOUNT WHICH FALLS TO THE LOT OF A CULTIVATED MAN OF OUR UNHAPPY 19TH CENTURY.

Nietzsche was trying to uproot the last traces of Christianity; while Dostoyevsky, at heart a secret unbeliever, was passionately seeking for a Christian acceptance of life. Both share in a quest for the sense of being human at the extreme limit, and as such they are both pioneers of **Existentialism**.

The attempt to "become an insect" turns into a nightmare reality in the story *Metamorphosis* (1912) by **Franz Kafka** (1883–1924). Gregor Samsa's "real" transformation into a bug can be seen as the terminal materialization of sick consciousness.

Kafka anticipates the Existentialist condition of the "absurd" which can be seen in *The Outsider* (1946), a novel by **Albert Camus** (1913–60).

The Origins of "Good"

The idea of "Good" implicit in the slave ethic relies on the theory of **altruism**, i.e. any action which benefits others is an example of "goodness". Here again we see the self-effacing quality of the slave who sacrifices self-interest for the common good, comparable to the behaviour of certain insect communities.

Thus "Good" became identified with particular actions in the world. This fundamental error is perpetuated in the history of **naturalistic ethics**: theories which try to prove that goodness is inherent in a particular **action**.

THESE THEORIES CAN NEVER DEAL WITH CHANGES IN THE **CONTEXT** OF ACTIONS, E.G. "IT IS GOOD TO SHOW MERCY".

THIS PROPOSITION WILL NOT BE VERY PLAUSIBLE WHEN APPLIED TO AN ENEMY WHOSE FIRST CONCERN IS TO KILL ME AT ALL COSTS!

Altruistic actions will no doubt be commended by their recipients. But why should the doers of these actions have thought they were "Good" in the first place?

The origins of the "Good" must lie in another direction which requires an **historical** awareness of our moral development. Here, Nietzsche reminds us of the ancient lordly right of bestowing names upon things – an expression of the ruler's power. "They say, 'This **is** that or that'; they seal off each thing and action with a sound and thereby take symbolic possession of it."

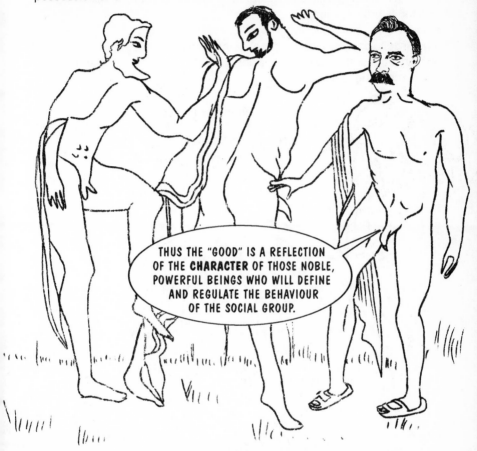

THUS THE "GOOD" IS A REFLECTION OF THE **CHARACTER** OF THOSE NOBLE, POWERFUL BEINGS WHO WILL DEFINE AND REGULATE THE BEHAVIOUR OF THE SOCIAL GROUP.

The linguistic origin or **etymology** of the word "good" also shows its association with the stronger, more powerful group. In German, the words *schlecht* (bad) and *schlicht* (simple) are closely related. "For a long time the first term (*schlecht*) was used interchangeably with the second (*schlicht*) without any contemptuous connotation as yet, merely to designate the commoner as opposed to the nobleman." The idea of "Bad" came to be associated with notions of "common", "plebeian" or "base". Another example of the "creation of values" which only the noble spirit is capable of doing.

The Ascetic Ideal

Finally, let us try to answer the question of why the slave ethic is so successful. Why does the ascetic ideal of the priestly caste still possess such a terrible fascination for so many? The answer lies in the function of the ascetic teaching: "The ascetic ideal arises from the protective and curative instinct of a life that is degenerating and yet fighting tooth and nail for its preservation."

The ascetic priest is a comforter of human suffering. He offers an explanation for that suffering, making the sickness easier to bear; he gives **meaning** to it.

Thence follows the slave ethic. **Resentment** now finds a target, **conscience** is born, **guilt** takes effect.

Herein lies the power of the ascetic ideal; that it provides a meaning for existence – its only meaning so far. As such, we can only admire this achievement, and with it, the great **act of will** required to create such a system (albeit a sick one!).

In short, it is fatally **anti-life**. We have to conclude that it represents "a will to nothingness, a revulsion from life, a rebellion against the principal conditions of living".

The Triumph of Nihilism

The ascetic ideal and the ethics of the slave constitute for Nietzsche the greatest malady ever to have afflicted mankind (but entirely of our own creation!). He describes this system as **decadent** (literally "declining", "falling away").

The human need to find meaning in existence – even a negative meaning which denies the possibility of human improvement – leads us to the last line of Nietzsche's *Genealogy of Morals*.

The Anti-Christ

In his final year of complete lucidity (1888), Nietzsche completed two short works, *Twilight of the Idols* and *The Anti-Christ*. The latter is a sustained attack on the Christian ethic. In the foreword, Nietzsche remarks that its readers will require "courage for the forbidden" and "new eyes for the most distant things". Its proposed subtitle was "The Revaluation of all Values".

Twilight of the Idols well exemplifies Nietzsche's method of irony, philosophizing "with the hammer as with a tuning-fork". Here we find his famous paradox: "I fear we are not getting rid of God because we still believe in grammar . . ." This, in a few words, sums up Jacques Derrida's programme of *deconstruction*, that is, his attack on the Western tradition of "logocentrism". Nietzsche had always criticized the illusion that the existence of a word guarantees the truth of what the word refers to.

WE DO NOT MERELY DESIGNATE THINGS BY WORDS, BUT WE ORIGINALLY BELIEVE THAT THROUGH THEM WE GRASP WHAT IS **TRUE** IN THINGS.

Nietzsche also provides the source of another influential "postmodern" idea, Jean Baudrillard's notion of the *simulacrum* or the nullification of reality itself as hyper-reality. In a single page, Nietzsche traces the six stages: *How the "Real World" at last Became a Myth*. The "real world" (or the "History of an Error") which begins with Plato's Idealism, and passes on to Christianity, Kantianism, Logical Positivism, becomes increasingly **unknown**, until it is of no use, superfluous, and is finally abolished. "We have abolished the real world: what world is left? The apparent world perhaps? . . ."

Recognition at Last?

At this point, Nietzsche's writings were slowly gaining ground in Europe. The eminent French critic **Hippolyte Taine** (1828–93) responded enthusiastically to *Beyond Good and Evil* (another book printed at Nietzsche's own expense). In Denmark, another influential critic and historian, **Georg Brandes** (1842–1927), lectured on Nietzsche's philosophy. The great Swedish playwright **August Strindberg** (1849–1912) was deeply impressed by Nietzsche's ideas.

Nietzsche's letters to Brandes and Strindberg at the close of 1888 frankly reveal the perilously megalomaniac state of his mind. *Ecce Homo*, the last book Nietzsche wrote (1888), takes its title from Pilate's greeting to Jesus in his crown of thorns (St. John's Gospel, 19:5). "Mankind can begin to have fresh hopes only now that I have lived." And in a letter to Strindberg (7 December 1888), he wrote . . .

Nietzsche had compensated too long for his extreme loneliness and the neglect that his work suffered. Finally, before he paid the price of complete mental breakdown, he saw himself as the Anti-Christ – or the anti-Christian saviour.

On 31 December 1888, he sent a message to Strindberg.

Nietzsche's Breakdown

"Apart from the fact that I am decadent, I am also the reverse of such a creature." (from *Ecce Homo*) It can be said that each of Nietzsche's books is a stage in the duel between these two antagonists inside himself. He deliberately set out to discover every possible "decadent" trait in himself and then immediately prescribed the antidote to combat each one. Hardness on himself contradicts the innate gentleness of Nietzsche's character.

On 3 January 1889, in the Piazza Carlo Alberto, Turin, he saw a coachman whipping an old horse. He embraced the animal, sobbed, and fainted. Nietzsche had finally lost his sanity.

The degree of Nietzsche's insanity is still a matter of debate. His friend, the eminent professor of philology, Johannes A. Overbeck, has left an interesting comment: "I could not entirely resist the thought that Nietzsche's illness was simulated – an impression derived from my long-standing experience of his habit of taking on many different masks."

There even exists a book, *My Sister and I*, allegedly written by Nietzsche in his last years at Weimar where his sister Elizabeth Förster-Nietzsche cared for him. She had returned from Paraguay in 1895, six years after her husband's suicide.

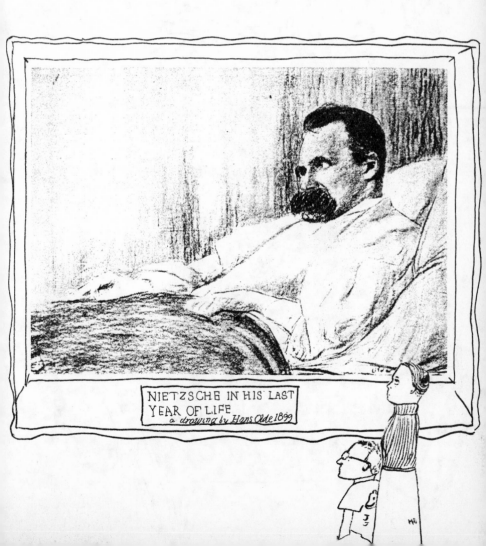

NIETZSCHE IN HIS LAST YEAR OF LIFE
a drawing by Hans Olde 1899

Nearly twelve years after his breakdown, on 25 August 1900, Nietzsche died of pneumonia at Weimar.

In a short eulogy at the graveside, Peter Gast, perhaps unwittingly, fulfilled the first of Nietzsche's premonitions.

Nietzsche and the Nazis

Nietzsche's sister Elizabeth rejected Peter Gast's attempt to edit the many unpublished manuscripts and took complete control of the archive of her brother's work.

Elizabeth supervised the publication of the archive. Her nationalist sentiments ensured Nietzsche's place in the emerging politics of German imperialism in the First and Second World Wars.

Shortly before her death in 1935, Elizabeth thanked Hitler for the honour he had "graciously bestowed on my brother".

It is an irony of history that Nietzsche's outspoken hatred of racism in general, and anti-Semitism in particular, should have been so effectively suppressed by his greatest proponents – the Nazis.

Later, at the Nuremberg trials of Nazi war criminals (1946), Nietzsche was cited as a major figure of Nazi ideology. Nietzsche himself seems to have dreaded and yet prophesied this total misrecognition of his ideas, as he does (ironically enough) in a letter to his sister from Venice, June 1884.

Politicians, as Nietzsche had observed, are more concerned with expedience than truth, and Hitler himself unashamedly agreed with this in his book, *Mein Kampf* (*My Struggle*, 1925–6).

The Case for the Defence

Leaving aside the complexities of Nazi ideology, the question of **racism** is perhaps the simplest way of separating Nietzsche from Hitler. Compare Hitler's pronouncements in *Mein Kampf* with Nietzsche's view in a letter to his sister from Nice, 26 December 1887.

On the related issue of **nationalism** Nietzsche is quite clear. Few writers have had less respect for their country and its politics. A letter from Switzerland, 12 May 1887, will suffice to show this. "I feel kinship only with the most cultivated French and Russian people, but not at all with the so-called distinguished *élite* among my own countrymen, who judge everything from the principle: 'Germany above everything' . . ."

LET HIM COME TO ZARATHUSTRA WHO HAS UNLEARNED THE LOVE OF HIS PEOPLE BECAUSE HE HAS LEARNED TO LOVE MANY PEOPLES.

In fact, Zarathustra preaches the **international creed**.

Nietzsche and Psychoanalysis

Both Marx and Freud have in common with Nietzsche the "method of suspicion". Their analyses of culture and consciousness present a history of **false-consciousness**.

Freud's admiration for Nietzsche shows in his development of key ideas.

All instincts which do not find a vent outside oneself turn inwards.
Genealogy of Morals

All suppressed truths become poisonous.
Zarathustra

SUCH REMARKS ARE CLEARLY THE BEGINNINGS OF MY THEORY OF **NEUROSIS**.

The Freudian notion of **repression** is also anticipated in Nietzsche's analysis of pride in *Beyond Good and Evil*.

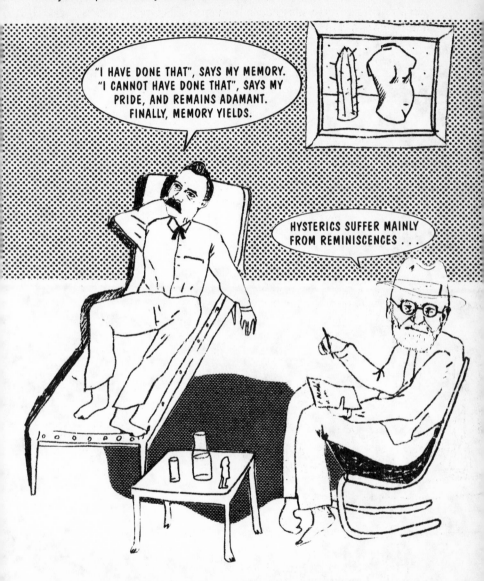

Freud's **pathological** orientation – the idea that only in the study of the abnormal person can we learn the true nature of "normal" psychology – is reflected in Nietzsche's proposition in *Human, All Too Human* that: "Deviating natures are of the utmost importance wherever there is to be progress."

On numerous topics, we find the anticipation of psychoanalytic thinking.

Religion: *God is a gross answer . . .*
at bottom merely a gross prohibition
for us: you shall not think!

Humour:
Wit is the epitaph of an emotion.
Human, All Too Human

Sexuality: *The degree and kind of a person's*
sexuality reaches up into the topmost
summit of his spirit.
Beyond Good and Evil

Dreaming: *Either one does not dream*
at all or one dreams in an interesting manner.

Indeed, without his psychological critique, Nietzsche's work on culture and morality would not have been possible. Such a critique must draw on the author's own psychic reality if it is to have real insight. Here, Nietzsche paid the full price for his self-knowledge. "When I have looked into my *Zarathustra*, I walk up and down in my room for half an hour, unable to master an unbearable fit of sobbing."

The price of great despair is revealed in these two sentences from Nietzsche's draft notes to *Will to Power* (1886–8).

Wittgenstein: Linguistic Philosophy

20th century philosophical interest in language has found inspiration in Nietzsche's writings. The later philosophy of **Ludwig Wittgenstein** (1889–1951) uses the idea of meaning as the **use** of any utterance, stressing the **practical effects** of language.

This approach locates meaning in the changing **relationship** between thought and action and rejects the idea of meaning as something fixed and timeless, or merely a property of logical analysis, as Nietzsche had already foreseen in his *Early Greek Philosophy* (1873).

THE MAJESTY OF TRUTH IS NOT SCALED BY THE ROPE LADDER OF LOGIC.

. . . ANYONE WHO UNDERSTANDS ME EVENTUALLY RECOGNIZES MY PROPOSITIONS AS NONSENSICAL, WHEN HE HAS USED THEM – AS STEPS – TO CLIMB UP BEYOND THEM. (HE MUST, SO TO SPEAK, THROW AWAY THE LADDER AFTER HE HAS CLIMBED UP IT.)

from **Tractatus Logico-Philosophicus**, 6.54 (1922)

These changing relationships, or "forms of life", undermine language as "literal" expression, and show it as a more complex relationship of metaphors, similes, metonyms and poetic devices. Thus "literal meaning" is simply figurative language whose complexities have been forgotten, as Wittgenstein reminds us in his *Philosophical Investigations* (1953), and as we see in Nietzsche's picture of language.

TO IMAGINE A LANGUAGE IS TO IMAGINE A FORM OF LIFE.

TRUTHS ARE ILLUSIONS, WHOSE ILLUSORY NATURE HAS BEEN FORGOTTEN, METAPHORS THAT HAVE BEEN USED UP AND HAVE LOST THEIR IMPRINT — THAT NOW OPERATE AS MERE METAL AND NO LONGER AS COINS.

Heidegger and Nietzsche

In his essay *The Word of Nietzsche*, **Martin Heidegger** (1889–1976) presents Nietzsche as the greatest critic of the Western metaphysical tradition exemplified by Plato. "Through the overturning of metaphysics accomplished by Nietzsche, there remains for metaphysics nothing but a turning aside into its own inessentiality and disarray."

This tradition, seen as the rise and development of **nihilism**, is at a turning-point (the postmodern crisis?).

TO GO BEYOND THIS STAGE REQUIRES FOR NIETZSCHE A NEW RELATIONSHIP WITH **TRUTH**, AND FOR ME A NEW RELATIONSHIP WITH **BEING** AS WELL.

What does **Being** (*Sein* in German) mean for Heidegger? It means: "What is given to thinking to think." In other words, Being goes beyond any **system** of thought. But "going beyond" does not imply **transcendence** in the ultimate significance of man's existence in the world – a question vitally important to Nietzsche.

Being should be understood in the sense of **horizon**, which, like the problem of time itself, is resistant to philosophizing – hence the title of Heidegger's key work, *Sein und Zeit* (Being and Time), 1927.

An important strand of Heidegger's thought comes from his teacher **Edmund Husserl's** (1859–1938) method of **Phenomenology** (an austere inspection of the mind's logical contents) which Heidegger uses to investigate extreme states of mind: anxiety, concern, authenticity, nothingness. And this has allied Heidegger – against his wishes – to **Existentialism**.

Jean-Paul Sartre: Existentialism

The first principle of Existentialist philosophy according to **Jean-Paul Sartre** (1905–80) is that "existence precedes essence". By this he means that we each have individually to determine our identity. "Human nature" is indeterminate until it is realized by acts of free choice. Thus, the first fact we encounter is that of our **existence**, from which follows a "terrible freedom" in which we are condemned to make choices at every moment of our life.

EVEN THE DECISION TO MAKE NO CHOICE IS A CHOICE!

Le Néant

Le Néant is Sartre's French borrowing of Heidegger's *Das Nichts*, both meaning nothingness or an objectless state of anxiety.

Indeed, our "nature" too is nothing until a character is chosen. Only this way can we live authentically in Existentialist terms. The Nietzschean emphasis on the fundamental role of the **will** provides the bedrock of Existential thought – a philosophy of willed freedom and the inescapable fact of human choice.

Derrida: Deconstruction

Nietzsche's call for a "revaluation of all values" is a prefigurement of **Jacques Derrida**'s strategy of disruption in philosophy which he named **deconstruction**. Deconstruction is a notoriously slippery term: it is in fact *undecidable*. Derrida (b. 1930) himself has suggested that deconstruction should be described as a "suspicion against thinking, *what is the essence of?*" In this sense, it is an attack on the Western metaphysical tradition of *logocentrism* which seeks a single, timeless and fixed point of origin for truth. Such a declaration of war finds its precedent in Nietzsche's "principle of suspicion".

EVERY WORD IS A PRECONCEIVED JUDGEMENT.

MY INTENTION IS TO MAKE ENIGMATIC WHAT ONE THINKS ONE UNDERSTANDS BY WORDS.

Nietzsche's writings in their use of irony, playful paradox and disruption of classical logic are a model for Derrida's proposal of deconstruction. Both thinkers agree that the age-old "dream of a foundational truth" must finally be relinquished.

If one can truly understand why there cannot be a "Nietzschean" philosophy, then it will become clear why Derrida insists that deconstruction must not become deconstruction**ism**. It must not surrender to becoming a rule-governed method, a *foundation*. "I'd say that deconstruction loses nothing from admitting that it is impossible."

163

Foucault: Knowledge and Power

The most influential heir to Nietzsche's "genealogical" method of conceptual analysis is the French philosopher and historian of ideas, **Michel Foucault** (1926–84). His *magnum opus*, *The Order of Things* (subtitled "An Archaeology of the Human Sciences") perfectly reflects the Nietzschean picture of knowledge as an essentially **human** project to produce order from chaos.

AS THE ARCHAEOLOGY OF OUR THOUGHT EASILY SHOWS, MAN IS AN INVENTION OF RECENT DATE. AND ONE PERHAPS NEARING ITS END.

Foucault emphasizes that our present mode of thinking about ourselves is finite. This finds its first expression in Nietzsche's remark on philosophers in *Human, All Too Human*. ". . . they involuntarily think of 'man' as an *aeterna veritas*, as something that remains constant in the midst of all flux, as a sure measure of things. Everything the philosopher has declared about man is, however, at bottom no more than a testimony as to the man of a very limited period of time."

Foucault's Micro-Histories

Foucault considered the relation of genealogy to history and philosophy in his essay, *Nietzsche, Genealogy, History* (1971). We remember that Nietzsche had called for a study of "other histories" that are the anonymous facts of our daily lives. Foucault fulfilled Nietzsche's demand by writing the micro-histories of madness, sexuality and punishment.

ALL THAT WHICH HAS GIVEN COLOUR TO EXISTENCE HAS HAD NO HISTORY . . . WHERE IS THERE A HISTORY OF LOVE, AVARICE, ENVY, CONSCIENCE, PIETY, CRUELTY? EVEN A COMPARATIVE HISTORY OF JUSTICE, OR EVEN ONLY PUNISHMENT, IS COMPLETELY LACKING.

TO WRITE SUCH HISTORIES REQUIRES A **TRANSGRESSION** OF THE TRADITIONAL BOUNDARIES OF THOUGHT – A RADICAL RETHINKING OF WHAT WE MEAN BY "KNOWLEDGE" IN RELATION TO "POWER".

Foucault's achievement has been to expand and document Nietzsche's central concern: the **Will to Power** as the primary ground of human discourse – and particularly, the discourse of **knowledge**.

. . . TRUTH ISN'T OUTSIDE POWER . . . TRUTH IS OF THE WORLD: IT IS PRODUCED BY VIRTUE OF MULTIPLE CONSTRAINTS. AND IT INDUCES THE REGULAR EFFECTS OF POWER. EACH SOCIETY HAS ITS RÉGIME OF TRUTH, ITS "GENERAL POLITICS" OF TRUTH: THAT IS, THE TYPES OF DISCOURSE IT HARBOURS AND CAUSES TO FUNCTION AS TRUE.

Nietzsche and Postmodernism

The shadow of Nietzsche lies across much postmodern theory. **Jean-François Lyotard** (b. 1924) has famously characterized the postmodern condition (1979) as a disordering of the traditional "grand narratives" of Western progressive thought. The idea of Truth itself has been "de-centred". But now that the "will to truth has been forced to examine itself", we are experiencing a proliferation of philosophical and critical theories of epidemic proportions. Nietzsche himself would not have approved.

(Postmodern) Theory Wars

Jean Baudrillard (b. 1929) simultaneously analyzes and exemplifies this dangerous event: the explosion of theory. His apocalyptic writings both create and annihilate their object. These "theory wars", like military wars, rage around us, just as Nietzsche foretold in *Ecce Homo*.

. . . ALL THE POWER-STRUCTURES OF THE OLD SOCIETY HAVE BEEN BLOWN APART — THEY ALL RESTED ON A LIE: THERE WILL BE WARS SUCH AS THERE HAVE NEVER YET BEEN ON EARTH.

IT IS NO LONGER RELEVANT TO SAY THE REAL WORLD "EXISTS". NO SYSTEM OF REPRESENTATION OR ANALYSIS CAN REFER TO THE REALITY.

How does Baudrillard deal with "the lie" at the basis of the social power- structure?

The Simulacrum

In 1981, Baudrillard pronounced reality **dead**. "The real" is now only **simulated** by signs. We have seen Nietzsche's preview of this idea of the real world's "disappearance" (see pages 140–1). In a similar vein, Baudrillard traces the four stages ("genealogy") of signs that lead to the postmodern extinction of reality.

*1. The sign is the **reflection** of a basic reality.*

*2. Next it **masks** and **perverts** a basic reality.*

*3. Then it marks the **absence** of a basic reality.*

*4. Finally it bears **no relation** to any reality whatever – it is its own pure simulacrum.*

Welcome to **hyper-reality**!

Postmodern Hyper-reality

The epidemic amounts of postmodern theory, the paranoid sense of existing in a hyper-real vacuum, are not simply the outcome of academic "theory wars". They reflect a desperate vertigo, an attempt to keep up with the postmodern revolutions in cosmology, genetics and digital technology.

Here is an example. In February 1997, a sheep (appropriately named Dolly) was cloned at the Roslin Institute in Edinburgh.

Professor Rotblat left the Los Alamos A-bomb project in 1944, morally anguished at the mass destruction he had helped to unleash. He devoted himself to medical research and anti-nuclear campaigning. He has condemned the genetic experiment of cloning as unethical.

We can credit Nietzsche with the foresight to question the "unlimited progress" of science. "Any truth which threatens life is no truth at all. It is an error." (See page 58)

Nietzsche has set us this vital question: "Knowledge – *for what purpose?*"

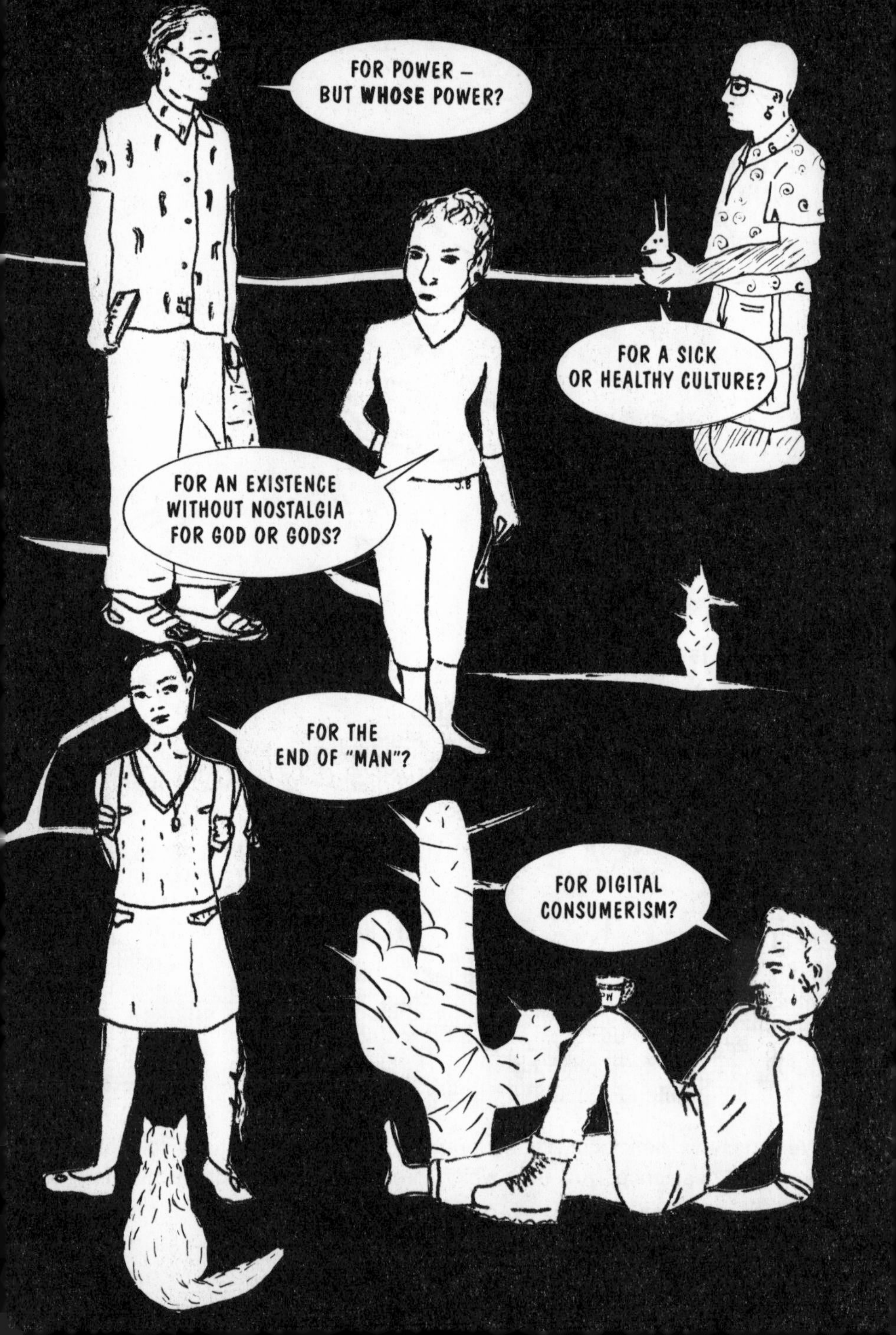

A Postmodern Fable

Nietzsche seems to have anticipated our postmodern blues in the following picture.

"The Don Juan of knowledge . . . He does not love the things he knows, but has spirit and appetite for the chase and intrigues of knowledge! – until at last there remains for him nothing left of knowledge to hunt down except the absolutely **detrimental**; he is like the drunkard who ends up drinking absinthe and aqua fortis. Thus in the end he lusts after Hell – it is the last knowledge that seduces him. And it too proves a disillusionment, like all knowledge! . . . for the whole universe has not a single crumb left to give to this hungry man."

Meanwhile, do we prefer "the void as our purpose, rather than be void of purpose . . ."?

Further Reading

Books by Nietzsche – selected texts

A Nietzsche Reader (Harmondsworth: Penguin, 1977). A useful selection from the most important texts, giving an overview of his ideas on religion, art, metaphysics, psychology and morality. The best one-volume collection.

The Genealogy of Morals (New York: Vintage, 1973). The most systematic and analytical of Nietzsche's writings on morality. Clear and unambiguous.

Thus Spake Zarathustra (Harmondsworth: Penguin, 1961). Drama, parable, metaphor and passion: the least systematic but arguably the most readable of all his writings.

Beyond Good and Evil (Harmondsworth: Penguin, 1973). Nietzsche's "prelude to a philosophy of the future". Great use of aphorism; widely read (and misunderstood).

Commentaries on his work

Nietzsche, by Walter Kaufmann (New Jersey: Princeton University Press, 1974). The first influential modern commentary, presenting him as a libertarian humanist.

Nietzsche's Voice, by H. Staten (Ithaca: Cornell University Press, 1990). The most sympathetic of the modern appreciations. Difficult but worthwhile.

Nietzsche: Life as Literature, by A. Nehemas (Cambridge, Mass.: Harvard University Press, 1985). A detailed and scholarly approach, of which Nietzsche may or may not have approved.

Friedrich Nietzsche: Philosopher of Culture, by Frederick Copleston (London: Search Press, 1975; New York: Barnes & Noble, 1975). As liberal and sympathetic as a Catholic Jesuit can be towards such a writer.

Reading Nietzsche, ed. R. Solomon and K. Higgins (Oxford: Oxford University Press, 1988). Contains useful commentaries on the reading of certain texts.

The New Nietzsche, ed. D. Allison (New York: Delta, 1977). An insight into contemporary French readings by Derrida, Deleuze and others. Difficult but provocative.

Nietzsche, by Michael Tanner (Oxford: Oxford University Press, 1994). Irascible, humorous and full of insights. The best modern short commentary.

Biographies

The Tragic Philosopher, by F. Lea (London: Athlone Press, 1993). Highly stylized and biased, but containing much interesting detail.

Nietzsche on Tragedy, by M. Silk and J. Stern (Cambridge: Cambridge University Press, 1981). A biographical commentary, full of useful insights.

Acknowledgements

Laurence Gane would like to thank Chris Horrocks, Michael Tanner, Richard Appignanesi and the ghost of Michel Foucault. Supreme gratitude to Gabrielle for her undying provocation and Nietzschean fortitude.

Kitty Chan would like to thank the following people for their help, contributions and support throughout the production of this book: Ann Course, Hannah Dyson, Simon, John, Mark and Jim for making the light box, Martin Chan, Yim Hing, Sik Jong and Patrick Furse.

Typesetting by **Wayzgoose** and **Nancy White**
Speech balloons by **Patrick Furse**

Laurence Gane read philosophy at University College and Kings College London. He was a founder member of the London Film-Makers Co-Op. He teaches at the Royal College of Art in London and lives in Snowdonia.

Kitty Chan graduated from the Royal College of Art and is currently working as a freelance illustrator in London.